AMERICA FOR SALE

A Collector's Guide to Antique Advertising

Price Guide included

Douglas
Congdon-Martin

1469 Morstein Road, West Chester, Pennsylvania 19380

Dedication

To Stewart Martin, and Zachary, Nicholas, and Chapin Hansen

DISTRIBUTING SHIP CARGO OF STANDARD BUGGIES COAST OF AUSTRALIA

Columbus Buggy Co., paper poster depicting Aborigines from Australia riding the ostriches that pull the buggy. Cincinnati Litho Co., 34″ x 23.5″. *Courtesy of Oliver's Auction Gallery.*

Published by Schiffer Publishing, Ltd.
1469 Morstein Road
West Chester, Pennsylvania 19380
Please write for a free catalog.
This book may be purchased from the publisher.
Please include $2.00 postage.
Try your bookstore first.

We are interested in hearing from authors
.with book ideas on related subjects.

Copyright © 1991 by Schiffer Publishing, Ltd.
Library of Congress Catalog Number: 91-65650.

Printed in the United States of America.
ISBN: 0-88740-333-6

Front cover photo:
Embossed tin advertising sign which sold at auction in July, 1990 for $85,000. Campbell Soup created a controversy by using the American flag in this way, and the fury it engendered may account for the few known examples. Manufactured by the Standard Advertising Company of Coshocton, Ohio. 40″ x 26″. *Courtesy of Oliver's Auction Gallery.*

Title page photo:
Paper Budweiser sign with original wood frame, copyright 1907. Kaufmann & Strauss Co., New York, 38.5″ x 23″. *Courtesy of The Hug Collection.*

Contents

Acknowledgements

This book was made possible by the generous cooperation of many collectors and dealers. They include: Becky & Bob Alexander, The Olde Mercantile Store, Rogers, Arkansas; Sue & Ted Allen, Hadley Antique Center, Amherst, Massachusetts; Herb & Elaine Aschendorf; Kit Barry, Kit Barry Collection, Brattleboro, Vermont; Dave Beck, Beck's Ltd., Mediapolis, Iowa; Betty Blair, Apple Attic, Jackson, Ohio; Robert Blake, Bygones by Blake, Jackson, Michigan; Renee Braverman, R.A.G. Time, New York, New York; Mike & Doris Brown, Brownsville Station Antiques, Louisville, Kentucky; Dick and Katie Bucht, Bear Trap Antiques, Lionel Lakes, Wisconsin; Harold & Elsie Edmondson, Cherry Acres Antiques, Traverse City, Michigan; Joe & Sue Ferriola, Rare-Bits Antiques, Stevens, Pennsylvania; Frank & Betty Lou Gay; Fil and Robbie Graff, The Brewer's Monk, Naperville, Illinois; Dennis & Gloria Healzer, Shawnee, Kansas; Boyd A. Hitchner, Hitchner-Morrison, Haddonfield, New Jersey; Vic & Tom Hug, The Hug Collection, Lorain, Ohio; Barbara Hyman, Crown Antiques, Pittsburgh, Pennsylvania; Judith Jones, Signs of the Times, Athens, Ohio; David Justice & Beth Fraser, Signs of the Times, Mexico Beach, Florida; Bob & Marilou Kay, Bob Kay's Antiques, Batavia, Illinois; John & Dale Kemler, Alma, Michigan; Ron Koehler & Cindy Marsh, Koehler Bros. Inc.-The General Store, Lafayette, Indiana; Kim and Mary Kokles, Garland, Texas; Dave Lowenthal, Hog Wild Antiques, Canyon County, California; Gary Metz, Muddy River Trading Company, Roanoke, Virginia; Jay & Joan Millman, Quality Antique Advertising, Denver, Pennsylvania; Oliver's Auction Gallery, Kennebunk, Maine; Phil Perdue, Louisville, Kentucky; Bill Powell, Bill Powell American Arts, Franklin, Tennessee; Herbert Ramsey, Hutchinson, Kansas; Road Runner Antiques; Stan Rosenwasser, Seroco Antiques, Brinklow, Maryland; Frank & Barbara Speal, Frank's Antiques, Hiliard, Florida; Don Stuart, House of Stuart, Jinsen Beach, Florida; Ted & Donna Tear, The Old General Store, New Baltimore, Michigan; Bob Thomas, Synthiana, Kentucky; Marcia and Bob Weissman, Neat Olde Things, Stewartsville, New Jersey; Al Wilson, Las Vegas, Nevada.

Neal Wood of L & W Books graciously invited us to two national advertising shows in Indianapolis, where some of the leading dealers in antique advertising gather twice each year. He gave us the space and the introductions that made our job enjoyable and easy. Donna Armstrong-Meyers, Administrative Assistant at the Coshocton Ohio Area Chamber of Commerce, and Christy Tharp, of the Coshocton Public Library, lent their assistance in researching the development of the specialty advertising industry in Coshocton.

Here at home, Bob Biondi was of great assistance in gathering information and photography. Kate Dooner, our newest team member, also contributed her skill and energy. As usual, Ellen J. (Sue) Taylor designed the book with skill and artistry.

It always amazes me that, although I began as a complete stranger to most of the people mentioned above, they welcomed me into their worlds, shared their collections and information with me, and made me feel like an old friend. I hope one day to be just that. Thank you.

Douglas Congdon-Martin
West Chester, Pennsylvania

Introduction

America for Sale: A Collector's Guide to Antique Advertising covers the century that began about 1880. It is a small segment of the history of advertising, but is exciting for its variety and artistry. It is the century of the information explosion, where countless merchants, pitchers, and hawkers vied for the attention of the consumer. This meant that these were creative times in advertising.

The results of this creativity have been called the "poor man's" art. Beautifully designed posters with illustrations by some of America's foremost artists, Maxfield Parrish, N.C. Wyeth, Philip R. Goodwin, Norman Rockwell, and others, touted everything from corn flakes to automobiles, and shot guns to soup. The beauty of their work insured that it received a place of prominence in the store or marketplace, and that prominent location would boost sales, which is, after all, the purpose of the whole endeavor.

But advertising during the century involved more than posters. It also included brilliant signs that pushed the typographical arts to new limits. Tin and enamel signs could endure the elements, so they were often seen on the outside of buildings where they drew the attention of passers-by and helped the companies establish brand recognition and loyalty. Their durability also meant that they would survive through the years to become highly collectible today.

The advertisers' creativity was seen not only in the illustrative and graphic arts, but in the varieties of form. Anywhere a blank space was found was an opportunity for the advertiser. From large spaces to small, from the sides of barns and buildings to the sides of pin knives and memo pads, the advertiser's message could be found.

With the growth of advertising over the years there has been an accompanying growth of complaints about the pervasiveness of advertising, about how commercial everything has become. Perhaps it is true, but I suspect that beneath the complaining there has always been a certain fascination with advertising. It has been a part of our lives. It has informed, excited, ignited our dreams, and made people look toward and work for the future.

Now it is also a way to look at the past. In these pages you will see the advertiser's art as it has developed over the century. You will feel its persuasiveness and seductivity. And you will come to understand why it is so avidly collected and cherished today. Enjoy!

English wall scene, 1830. From a U.S. Patent Office publication, c. 1895. Sackett & Wilhelms Litho Co, New York.

Following page:
Fine sign on linen for Romance Chocolates. The artist was Norman Rockwell, c. 1920. 20″ x 40″. *Courtesy of Oliver's Auction Gallery.*

ROMANCE
CHOCOLATES

Try the
ROMANCE "SELECTIONS" BOX
It contains Selections from 15 ROMANCE Packages

I.
A Brief History of Advertising

The Earliest Advertising

The birth of advertising may be hidden in the mists of pre-history. It is connected somehow with the gift of communication, the drive to be heard and understood, and the need to influence another's opinions and beliefs. In its earliest forms it was an oral art. Town criers and bellman would walk the streets, giving the latest news as well as announcing the goods and services that were being offered for sale in the community. James Wood traces these criers from ancient Greece and Rome to the streets of England and colonial America.[1] Perhaps their descendants live still in the form of television spokespersons and announcers.

English bell man, 1600. From a U.S. Patent Office publication, c. 1895. Sackett & Wilhelms Litho Co, New York.

The symbol for a barber shop has long been the red and white barber pole. Its origins lie in the days when the barber practiced bloodletting for its supposed healing powers. The blood soaked rags used to clean up the mess were hung on a pole to dry. *Courtesy of Frank and Betty Lou Gay.*

By putting the announcements in writing, the ancients found a way to keep the word constantly in front of their potential consumers. The Egyptians were known to have used papyrus for public advertisements and announcements. Signboards in ancient Greece were cited by Aristotle, and advertising for events like circuses and gladiator contests were pasted on walls throughout ancient Rome.

The more common form of advertising in the Roman world was the use of relief signs of terra cotta or stone which were set into the pilasters or the sides of the open shop fronts. These included symbols of the trade that occupied the store. For example, a goat was the sign of a dairy and a mule driving a mill was the sign of a baker.[2]

The use of symbology continued through the Middle Ages, into the nineteenth century, and on to the present. With a population that was largely illiterate, the symbols were the best way of telling the public what products or services they would find within. The trades each had their own symbol: a knife for the cutler, a shoe for the cobbler, a hand for the glover, a pair of scissors for the tailor. Each shop had its sign hanging in the street. In a densely populated area like London, the effect could be quite chaotic. Wood reports that Charles II became so annoyed with the signs that he declared that "no signs shall be hung across the streets shutting out the air and light of the heavens."[3]. It has been suggested that the profusion of signs contributed to the "frequent epidemical disorders" of London by obstructing the free circulation of air.

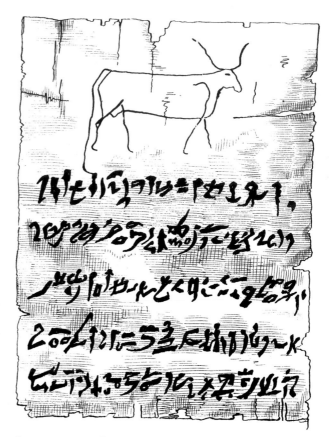

Egyptian papyrus advertisement, 2000 B.C. From a U.S. Patent Office publication, c. 1895. Sackett & Wilhelms Litho Co, New York.

Even tombstones have been used for advertisements. This one assures passers by that Jeremy Jobbins widow will carry on the business. England, circa 1800. From a U.S. Patent Office publication, c. 1895. Sackett & Wilhelms Litho Co, New York.

Advertising in America: Developing Technology

While it is hard to say when the first advertisement was used in America, the English traditions of criers and signs probably came ashore with the first settlers. There doubtless was a sign for a tavern or inn, or for one of the trades during the earliest colonial days.

The first newspaper advertisement appeared in the *Boston News-Letter*, America's second newspaper. It was published by John Campbell, Boston's postmaster, beginning in April, 1704. The first advertisement offered a reward for the return of two anvils "stolen from Mr. Shippen's wharf."[4]

Because of the difficulty in creating an image to be printed in the newspaper, most early advertisements were unillustrated, or carried only simple figures. The use of illustration in advertising came into its own with the development of trade cards in the late eighteenth century. Following the style of the English tradesmen's cards, they illustrated, often in detailed and beautiful engravings, the product or service being offered.

Technological developments in printing allowed for continuous improvement in both the quality and speed of printing in the early nineteenth century. The process of stereotyping was introduced, which used papier mâché molds to cast a whole page of type. This made it possible to make duplicate plates for printing and return the actual type to its case undamaged. The pantograph made it possible to copy illustrations to scale, though not in fine detail. The presses changed from wood to cast iron, and then to higher and higher levels of mechanization. In 1814, the *London Times* was producing complete copies of the newspaper at the rate of 1100 per hour, an unprecedented speed.[5]

This patented balloon with a printing press dropped advertisements over the country side. Perhaps that is where they got the name "flyers"! From a U.S. Patent Office publication, c. 1895. Sackett & Wilhelms Litho Co, New York.

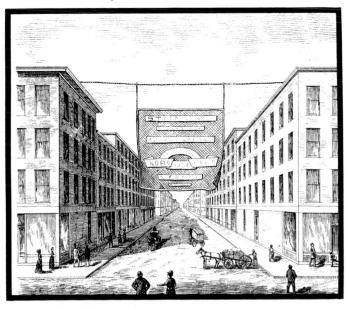

This banner design was among several to be patented and doubtlessly contributed to the clutter of advertising in the late nineteenth century. From a U.S. Patent Office publication, c. 1895. Sackett & Wilhelms Litho Co, New York.

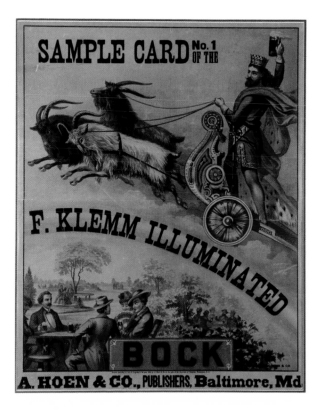

Sample Card No. 1 for the A. Hoen & Co., Publishers, Baltimore. Beautifully lithographed on paper, 27″ x 21″. *Courtesy of the Kit Barry Collection.*

9

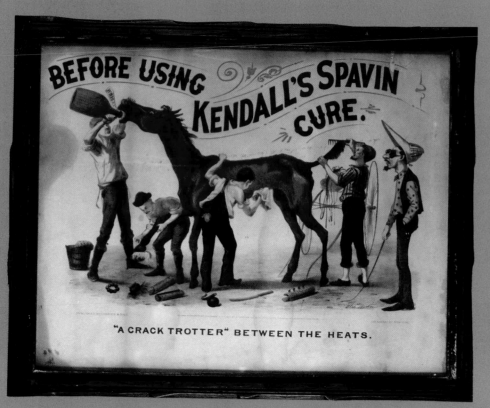

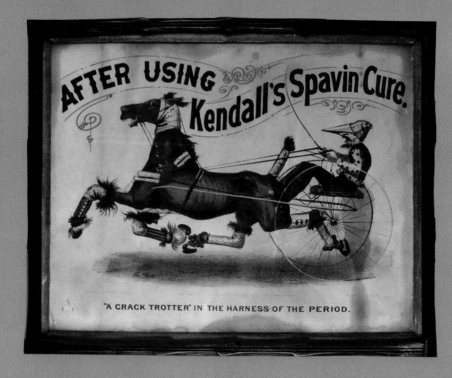

Great before and after advertising prints for Kendall's Spavin Cure. Currier & Ives, printed at the Nassau Street address, 20″ x 26″. Original frames. *Courtesy of Oliver's Auction Gallery.*

Opposite page:
American ingenuity showed itself in advertising as well as in other endeavors. Here we see just three of the thousands of advertising ideas that received patents in the last half of the nineteenth century. The wagon, patented in 1868, had an octagonal display that could carry a variety of advertisements through the streets. The mechanical smoker patented in 1877, was an early, and probably effective trade stimulator for the tobacconist. The use of the mirror in the drugstore display was enough to catch the consumers eye and attention. It was patented in 1882. From a U.S. Patent Office publication, c. 1895. Sackett & Wilhelms Litho Co, New York.

Electrotyping allowed the electrical engraving of a copper plate with great precision, thus increasing the quality and number of printed illustrations. The first electrotyped plate was used in America in 1840, in *Mapes's Magazine*, New York.

Meanwhile, in Bavaria, a playwright, Alois Senefelder, was experimenting with ways to publish his plays. He noticed that water did not stick to greased images on a stone and that greasy ink did. By using a grease pencil he could draw an image on a flat stone which would hold ink for printing. Its advantages were clear at once. It printed a positive image, while engraving printed in reverse. What the artist drew in black would print in black, though reversed. It was also a simple method. While engraving required trained people to copy the artists work on the copper plate, the simplicity of lithography allowed the artist to work directly on the stone. This gave the works the immediacy and personal touch of the artist.

Senefelder wrote a complete description of the lithographic process entitled *A Complete Course of Lithography*, which was published in English in 1819.[6]

Lithography flourished in Europe and England and was introduced in America in 1828. William and John Pendleton brought a M. DuBois to Boston from France. They also took on an apprentice from Roxbury, Massachusetts. His name was Nathaniel Currier. The rest is history.

Methods of color lithography using three colors superimposed by three stones, were developed in Europe in the 1830s. William Sharp introduced color lithography into his Boston printing firm in 1839.

As soon as they overcame the awkwardness of writing and drawing backwards, artists embraced the new process. It gave them the flexibility they needed to create and the capability of mass production, a combination that was not previously available to them.

With the development of color lithography a "craze for color" swept the country. As Hornung and Johnson report,

"Color suddenly blossomed out on posters and advertising ephemera of all kinds. Simultaneous with the perfecting of color lithography was an enormous demand in the market for anything printed in color that might serve a secondary purpose—or even a primary purpose: preservation in scrapbooks. Collecting colorful trifles for albums and memory books was as popular as stamp collecting is today."[7]

Louis Prang had the greatest impact on perfecting color lithography, and he was the one who coined the term "chromo-lithography." Prang was a refugee from Germany in 1848 and in 1856 went into business with Julius Meyer in Boston. Prang created drawings on stone and Meyer printed them. By 1867 Prang was in business for himself.

His work was beautiful, but tedious, involving the addition of one color impression upon another until the image was complete, often using as many as 32 stones. To do a 13" x 10" inch chromo of Eastman Johnson's *Barefoot Boy* took three months to prepare the stones and 5 months to print a thousand copies. According to Hornung and Johnson, Prang "felt that nobody could resist buying for five dollars an exact facsimile of a painting worth a thousand! He was right; he became enormously successful and world-famous."[8]

A turning point in American advertising followed on the heels of Prang's innovations and the Centennial Exhibition of Philadelphia in 1876. The posters, handbills, brochures, and flyers that were part of that celebration and the growing economy sent advertising into a flurry of activity and innovation. Barns, buildings, fences, and even cliffs became the sites of huge advertisements. Street car advertising was introduced and "business streets were so cluttered with hanging signs and banners that city authorities were obliged to regulate their size and number."[9]

Packaging and the Rise of Advertising in Tin

In the last twenty years of the 19th century, Americans also began to develop a taste for brand named, pre-packaged products, particularly foods. It was movement that benefited all concerned. The consumer avoided the often unsanitary conditions of buying their foods out of barrels or bins, and came to expect a consistency and quality from particular brands. The merchandiser no longer had the time consuming task of weighing and wrapping purchases, and could organize the store with orderly and efficient shelves. The producer could establish a brand name and brand loyalty, and use the lithographer's art to create attractive packaging to make their products stand out on the shelves of the stores. This, in turn, encouraged other advertising to establish the brand with the public. No longer would they go the store to buy corn flakes. Now they would seek Kellogg's Corn Flakes, and accept no substitutions.

One form this packaging took was in tin plated containers. Tinware had its roots in the middle ages, probably originating in Germany. Early examples are crude, limited by technology to thick sheets of iron. As the industry developed the tinware became more and more refined. Originally used primarily for household utensils like lamps, coffee pots, trays and other items, the first use to package a product was probably in the 1830s.[10] Then it was that Huntley and Palmers in Reading, England, created a biscuit tin that would keep the product fresh during transport and display. These were bulk tins, with printed paper or stenciled labels.

The early tin packaging was made by hand in a process so complicated that only a 100 could be made by a skilled tradesperson in a day. The industrial revolution brought significant changes in the tin trade. Machines could trim sheets to the required size and stamp tins from these sheets. This pressing process allowed for more intricate designs and embossed decorations. These fancier tins began to appear in the period from 1875-1885.[11]

Decorating tin was a problem. The shiny metallic surface was a difficult medium on which to print, and most of the early tins were plain or decorated with paper labels. The first limited successes in printing directly onto tin were in the mid-1860s, but using only the simplest designs and single colors.

Transfer printing was more successful. It was a process that had been used in the pottery industry for at least a century, and worked well with tin. The transfer was created by printing the image in reverse on paper, one color at a time. This was then applied by hand to a varnished tin and soaked so that the backing paper could be removed, leaving the printing on the tin.

In around 1869, processes for using lithography on tin were developed, though it is somewhat unclear who invented it. The first commercial use of lithography on tin began in 1877 at Huntley, Boorne, and Stevens in England. As with paper the first tin lithography utilized smooth stones for creating the images. These were replaced with thin zinc sheets introduced in 1895, making the process much simpler. By 1903 a rotary offset lithograph had been introduced into the tin industry which transferred the image from a

Game Tobacco store bin, c. 1915, Jno. J. Bagley & Co., Detroit. 7.5" H x 11.5" W x 7.5" D. *Courtesy of Gary Metz.*

rounded metal sheet to a rubber roller and then to the tin. Not only did this make the printing process faster, the introduction of the rubber transfer roller allowed the designer to stop working backwards.

After printing, the tins were heated in an oven to harden the printing and protect against cracking when the were embossed and cut. Because of the decoration, the cutting technology had to be made much more accurate than it had been with undecorated tin.

Peter Hornsby suggests that the tin sign grew out of the tin-box industry, and certainly the technology of one contributed to the other. But in America it was not long before a specialty of the tin sign grew up.

The Coshocton Experience

In 1875, Jasper Freemont Meek, a telegraph operator for the Pennsylvania Railroad, purchased the weekly newspaper in Coshocton, Ohio. To supplement the income produced by the paper, he did printing for the community. One history of the industry suggests that one day a salesman from New England came to town selling the merchants imitation greenbacks with advertising on the back. If a customer brought one of the greenbacks to the merchant's store he would receive a discount.[12]

The idea of novelty advertising appealed to Meek at once, and seeing a schoolboy lugging a stack of books, he developed the idea of printing advertising on something useful...a book bag. He made up a prototype with the slogan "Buy Cantwell Shoes" and proceeded to sell the idea to his friend Cantwell. An industry was born. Proceeding from the simple idea that if you give someone something useful, he will remember you when choosing a merchant.

Meek met with immediate success and soon nearly every child in Coshocton was sporting a new schoolbag, boldly imprinted with advertising. Soon horses joined the advertising parade, wearing Meek-produced blankets that kept the flies away, while advertising local businesses on a broad large surface.

In 1889 Meek's advertising business was separated from the newspaper, which it had long since outgrown. The operations were moved to an abandoned two-story factory building and renamed the Tuscarora Advertising Company. With the room and the vision for expansion, Meek enlarged the organization to include a national sales force.

H.D. Beach, another Coshocton businessman and the editor and publisher of the town's other newspaper, the *Democratic Standard*, saw the increased activity of Meek's presses and undertook to use his own more efficiently and profitably. He searched for items he could imprint, and beginning with a measuring stick found ways to run strips of wood through the press. The yard stick was followed by other useful wooden items including fly swatters, paint mixers, shoe horns, boot jacks, pencils, and more. Each was imprinted with an advertisement for the merchants to give to their customers.

Beach, too, found success in novelty advertising. Within a year he had sold the newspaper and organized the Standard Advertising Company. He leased a three story building in Coshocton and began production.

The competition between Meek and Beach kept them on the creative edge. One writer describes it as a nose to nose battle:

"When J.F. Meek came out with the latest thing in hats for horses, H.D. Beach came back with a

13

Kessler Brewery self-framing tin sign featuring the U.S. Gunboat Helena, c. 1900. Tuscarora Advertising Co., Coshocton, Ohio, 17″ x 23″. *Courtesy of The Olde Mercantile Store.*

painter's cap. Tuscarora Advertising's high-fashion carpenter's apron competed with Standard's carpenter's pencil. When Beach's customers flicked their nags with Standard buggy whips, Meek's comforted their steeds with Tuscarora horse blankets. Idea stimulated competitive idea and a vast assortment of clever specialty items poured out from Coshocton into all parts of the land. Bakers, bankers, brewers, butchers, book sellers, businesspeople in general reaped a rich harvest of good will and a grateful public naturally responded with enthusiasm."[13]

In the late 1880s and 1890s the product lines of both companies continued to expand. Meek printed his first advertising calendar in 1889 and the idea of an advertisement that would hang on the wall for a whole year immediately caught on. He was soon importing lithographed art from Germany to use on these calendars. He and Beach also produced wooden and metal signs, pocket books, memo books, card cases, desk ornaments, school tablets, pencil boxes, fans and countless other items.

Among the most sought after Coshocton items are the tin signs and trays that were produced there. Offset lithography was introduced to Meek's

Oval tray for Anheuser-Busch, 13″ long. Copyright Superb Graphics, 1900, by Standard Advertising Co. *Courtesy of Oliver's Auction Gallery.*

Rare die-cut tin stand-up sign for Windisch-Muhlhauser Brewing Co.,Cincinnati, Ohio. Meek & Beach, Coshocton, Ohio. *Courtesy of Mike and Doris Brown.*

Tuscarora plant in 1895, one of the earliest dates recorded anywhere in the world. Where the original stone plates were unable to print color on the metal, when the image was transferred to the rubber blanket beautiful tin signs were produced.

In 1899 the Tuscarora and Standard Advertising Companies merged and began operating together. The Meek and Beach Company was formally incorporated on March 23, 1901. No sooner was it done than the essential individualism of the two founders came to the fore. They agreed to separate and H.D. Beach sold out to Meek and bought a factory in New York which he moved to Coshocton. He called it the H.D. Beach Company, and it specialized in signs. It was incorporated in December, 1901.

Tin display for Stephenson Underwear, c. 1900. H.D. Beach Co., Coshocton, Ohio, 31″ x 15″ x 9.5″. Courtesy of Judith Jones, Signs of the Times.

Meek stayed put and, in 1905, renamed the company the Meek Company. In 1908 he gave up the leadership to go into retirement. Soon after Meek's retirement the company was renamed American Art Works. Incorporated in New Jersey in 1910 it was under the leadership of Charles R. Fredrickson, 35, who had represented the Meek and Beach Company in Kansas City with great success. In the three decades of Fredrickson's leadership American Art Works became a leading advertising manufacturer with an international clientele.

In 1930 American Art Works was purchased by American Colortype Co., but it was an uneasy alliance. When Jay Sadler Shaw and a group of his colleagues left Brown & Bigelow, a major advertising concern in St. Paul, Minnesota, they purchased the Calendar, Leather, and Specialty divisions in 1940. They renamed the company Shaw-Burton and it is now a division of JII/Sales Promotion Associates, which still operates in Coshocton on the site of the former Meek Tuscarora plant.[14] The tradition continues.

Outstanding Brookfield Rye self-framing tin sign. The Meek Co., Coshocton, Ohio, 33″ x 23″. *Courtesy of Oliver's Auction Gallery.*

"The Cock Fight," a 1912 tin sign for Rock Island Beer. American Art Works, Coshocton, Ohio, 20″ x 24″. *Courtesy of Oliver's Auction Gallery.*

Porcelain Enamel: An Old Art in a New Role

One of the most highly valued forms of advertising is the porcelain enamel sign, which was introduced at the beginning of the twentieth century. The techniques involved were not new. In fact, the ancient Egyptians used a form of enameling as early as the 14th century B.C. Enameling has enjoyed an almost uninterrupted history from then to the present. The first commercial enameling of cast iron happened in Bohemia around 1830. A few years later sheet iron and steel were successfully enameled, following some technological developments.

These early attempts involved a process of heating the metal until it was red hot, then dusting it with powdered enamel. This was then baked until the enamel melted to a smooth glass. While acceptable for some uses, this method did not give the control needed to create signs. Only when it was learned that clay may be used to keep the powdered enamel in suspension in water and cause it to adhere to the metal before firing, were the possibilities of enamel signs realized.[15]

The process begins by coating the metal with a slip of enamel suspended in a watery clay. This is done by dipping, or, in the case of larger pieces, spraying. This is allowed to dry and then fired at temperatures of 1450-1600 degrees Fahrenheit. This is the base coat to which other coats are added to create the color and design of the piece. One color is applied with each coat.

While the medium is very different, the technique is similar to that of the Japanese woodcut which was popular in the late 19th century. Joachim Richter connects the rise of the porcelain enamel to that popularity. The bold graphics, and strong solid colors used in juxtaposition to one another lent themselves to the medium of porcelain enamel and to the function of advertising.[16]

Joe's Fine Bread porcelain enamel sign, c. 1920s. 18″ x 14″. *Courtesy of David Justice and Beth Fraser.*

Porcelain enamel Welcome Borax Soap sign, 1920s. 10″ x 28″. DJ

Past and Present

The advertising of the last 100 years and more, gives us an insight into the past. It reveals the tastes of the people, how they thought, what they desired. It gives us a window on history, the world concerns, the technological developments that have shaped and molded it.

And it gives us a look at ourselves. While the media has changed over the years, the techniques have not. Advertisers are the cultural psychologists. They have keen insights into human nature. They know what we want and need, and they know how to make us want and need things we have never imagined.

Perhaps that is why advertising is so avidly collected. As much as any other part of our culture, and perhaps more, it carries the cultural history and identity of the American people. You can get a glimmer of that identity in our furniture and architecture. Our artists will open a bit more of it to you. But in advertising you get it all, directly and accurately. All the hopes and fears, desires and dreams of the American experience, and they're all for sale.

Footnotes

[1] James Playsted Wood, *The Story of Advertising,* New York, The Ronald Press Company, 1958), p. 18 ff.

[2] A U.S. Patent Office publication, circa 1895.

[3] Wood, *Op. cit.,* p. 24.

[4] *Ibid.,* p. 45

[5] Much of the technological history can be found in Clarence P. Hornung and Fridolf Johnson, *200 Years of American Graphic Art,* (New York: George Braziller, 1976)

[6] Alois Senefelder, *A Complete Course of Lithography* (New York: Da Capo Press, 1968)

[7] *Ibid.,* p. 75 ff.

[8] *Ibid.,,* p. 76

[9] *Ibid,* p. 93.

[10] Peter R.G. Hornsby, *Decorated Biscuit Tins* (West Chester, Schiffer Publishing, Ltd., 1984), p. 11

[11] *Ibid.,* p. 12

[12] The historical facts come from a paper published privately by Shaw-Barton, a direct descendant of the early advertising industry in Coshocton. No author is named.

[13] Shaw-Barton, *Ibid.,* p. 4.

[14] Ed Duling, "Coshocton Famous for its Advertising Trays," *Antique Week,* Vol. 24, No. 8 (Knightstown, Indiana: Mayhill Publications, May 20, 1991), p. 13

[15] R.M. Burns and W.W. Bradley, *Protective Coatings for Metals,* (New York: Reinhold Publishing Corporation, 1967), p.639 ff.

[16] Joachim F. Richter, *Antique Enamels for Collectors,* (West Chester: Schiffer Publishing Ltd., 1990), pp. 34-35.

II.
Signs and Posters

FOOD

Bread

Rainbo Bread tin sign, c. 1950s. 3″ x 18″. *Courtesy of Dave Beck.*

Tip-Top Bread tin sign, c. 1950s, manufactured by Barker Metal, Baltimore, Maryland. 3.5″ x 11″. *Courtesy of Dave Beck.*

Rainbo Bread tin door push. *Courtesy of Herbert Ramsey.*

Tin Sunbeam Bread sign dated 1961. 12" x 29.5". *Courtesy of Dave Beck.*

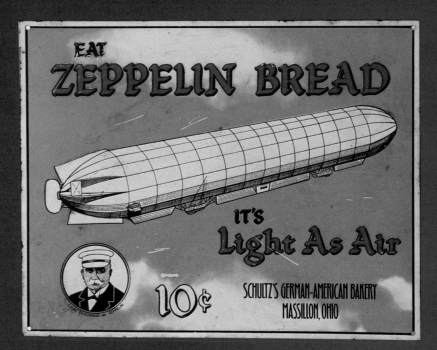

Tin Zeppelin Bread sign, c. 1910-1930. 11" x 14". *Courtesy of Mike and Doris Brown.*

Flour

DAKOTA MAID FLOUR

Dakota Maid Flour tin sign, 9.5" x 19.5". Circa 1920s.

Opposite page:
Three signs. TL: Two-sided early metal Fairy Soap sign. H.D. Beach Co., 18" x 12.25". TR: Extremely rare die-cut of Sleepy Eye Indian, manufactured by the Tuscarora Adv. Co. Litho. 9.75" x 13.25". B: Extremely rare Embossed tin Van Camp's Soup die-cut. Chas. Shonk Litho. 20.5" x 32". *Courtesy of Oliver's Auction Gallery.*

Hostess Flour, Gregory Roller Mills, Gregory, South Dakota. A tin sign from the 1940s, 20″ x 14″. *Courtesy of Dave Beck.*

Tin sign for Royal Patent Flour, the Nickel-Plate Milling Co., Painesville, Ohio. 11.25″ x 11.25″. *Courtesy of Dave Beck.*

Opposite page:
Sleepy Eye Flour tin sign, 24″ x 20″, c. 1910. *Courtesy of Gary Metz.*

Right:
Framed paper sign for Union Mills Flour, Farmer's Union & Milling Co., Stockton, California, c. 1910. 15″ x 19″. *Courtesy of The Hug Collection.*

Armour's Star Brand Mincemeat tin sign with wooden frame. Manufactured by Kaufmann & Strauss, New York, 31″ x 25″. *Courtesy of Joe and Sue Ferriola.*

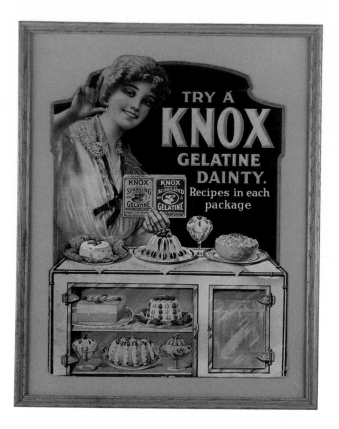

Knox Gelatine die-cut cardboard sign, c. 1918-1920. 21″ x 15.5″. *Courtesy of R.A.G. Time.*

Small, 6″ x 9″, Fleischmann's Yeast tin sign, manufactured by the Burack Co., Inc;. New York. *Courtesy of Jay and Joan Millman.*

Opposite page:
Wonderful embossed tin Frostlene cake frosting sign, 19.5″ x 27.5″. Lithographed by Standard Brands, Coshocton, Ohio. This sign was found in the wall of a house being torn down in Maine. *Courtesy of Oliver's Auction Gallery.*

Two-sided Clabber Girl Baking Powder tin sign, c. 1950s.
11.5" x 35". *Courtesy of Dave Beck.*

Ox-heart Chocolates and Cocoa enameled sign. Made by
Crump Printing Co., Buffalo, New York. 4.5" x 20".
Courtesy of Dave Beck.

Folding counter sign for three syrups. Cardboard 22" x 36".
Courtesy of Bob Thomas.

Other Foods

Opposite page:
Self-framed tin Grape-
nuts sign, 14" x 25"
image size. *Courtesy
of Oliver's Auction
Gallery.*

To school well fed on

Grape-Nuts

"There's a Reason"

Cardboard Kellogg's Toasted Corn Flakes sign, dated 1915. American Lithographic Co., New York, 20" x 11". *Courtesy of Gary Metz.*

Paper E.C. Corn Flakes sign, circa 1910-1919. The corn flakes were made in Quincy, Illinois and Buffalo, New York. The sign was manufactured by Umbdenstock & Porter Co., 219 S. Clinton St., Chicago. *Courtesy of Joe and Sue Ferriola.*

Armour's "Star" Ham tin sign, c. 1920s-1930s. W.D. Henderson Signs, Chicago, 13" x 19". *Courtesy of Dennis and Gloria Healzer.*

Hall, Luhrs, & Co., Corn-Fed Hogs tin sign manufactured by Kaufmann & Strauss Co., New York. Beneath the hog is the legend: "We live but once, why not live well and enjoy life?" Circa 1900, 14" x 19.75". *Courtesy of the House of Stewart.*

A great and desirable porcelain enamel sign for H.P Hood and Sons Milk, late 1930s. American Value's Enamel, 30" in diameter. *Courtesy of David Justice and Beth Fraser.*

Old Reliable Coffee two-sided tin sign. 24" x 16". *Courtesy of Gary Metz.*

Lion Coffee paper sign, 1893. Gast Lith. & Eng. Co., NY & Chicago, 31.5" x 22". *Courtesy of Gary Metz.*

White House Coffee and Tea, c. 1930s. Two-sided paper hanging sign, one side sepia-toned, the other with a second color added. 13″ x 10″. *Courtesy of Joe and Sue Ferriola.*

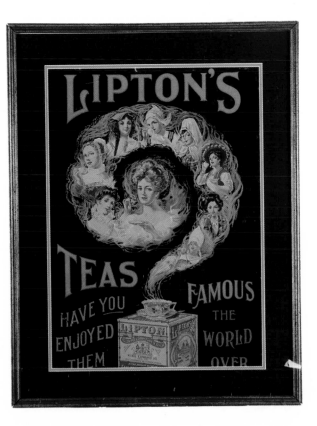

Lipton's Tea paper sign, c. 1901. 20″ x 14″. *Courtesy of R.A.G. Time.*

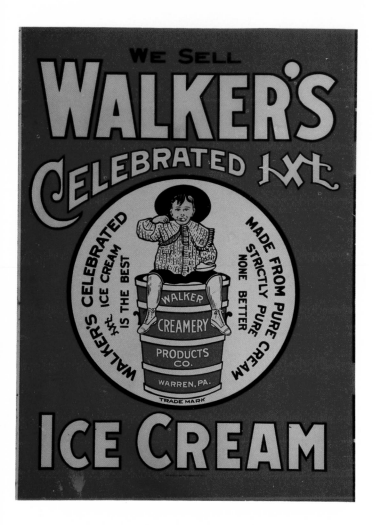

Two-sided Brown's Ice Cream sign, late 1920s. Porcelain enamel, 24″ x 20″. *Courtesy of David Justice and Beth Fraser.*

Two-sided tin Walkers Ice Cream sign. The Novelty Advertising Company, Coshocton, Ohio, 28″ x 20″ *Courtesy of Oliver's Auction Gallery.*

Tin Coons Ice Cream sign, c. 1918. The Kember-Thomas Co., Cincinnati, Ohio, 20″ x 59.5″. *Courtesy of Joe and Sue Ferriola.*

Paper sign for Hood's Penuchi Ice Cream. *Courtesy of Ted and Donna Tear.*

Embossed tin Peak's Candy sign, c. 1920s. 11.5″ x 27.5″. *Courtesy of Bob and Marilou Kay.*

Die-cut cardboard Zeno Gum sign, c. 1920s. 11.5″ x 6.5″. *Courtesy of Dennis and Gloria Healzer.*

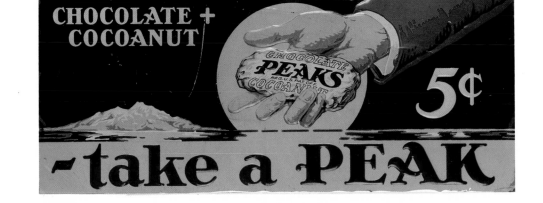

Paper sign for Little African Licorice Drops, c. 1910-1919. 11.5″ x 14.5″. *Courtesy of R.A.G. Time.*

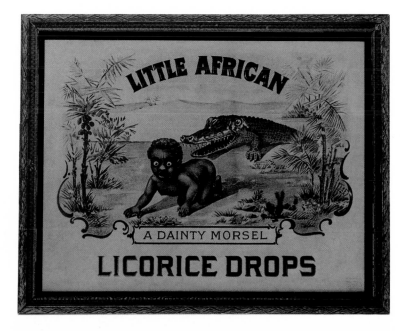

Oh Boy Gum tin sign, c. 1920s, the Goudey Gum Co., Boston & Chicago. 15.5" x 7.5". *Courtesy of Dave Beck.*

A nice die-cut tin sign for Woodward's Candy, John G. Woodward Co., Council Bluffs, Iowa. 14" x 10". *Courtesy of Dennis and Gloria Healzer.*

SOFT DRINKS

Ace Ginger Beer tin sign, c. 1920-1930. George Ackerman & Sons Co., Cincinnati, Ohio, 10" 27.5" *Courtesy of Dave Beck.*

B-1 Lemon-Lime Soda tin sign, c. 1930s. 3" x 16". *Courtesy of Dave Beck.*

Self-framing tin Big Boy sign, c. 1936-1942. Robertson Steel & Iron Company, Springfield, Ohio. 35″ x 11″. *Courtesy of Gary Metz.*

Brownie Chocolate Soda tin sign, c. mid-1930s. 40″ x14″. *Courtesy of Gary Metz.*

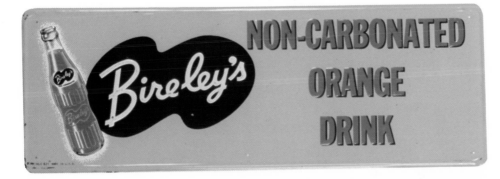

Tin sign for Bireley's Non-Carbonated Orange, c. 1950s. Stout Sign Co., 10″ x 28″. *Courtesy of Dave Beck.*

Buscho beverage sign, c. 1930. The Crown Cork and Seal Co., Baltimore, Maryland. 7" x 10". *Courtesy of Dave Beck.*

Canada Dry Beverages porcelain enamel sign, c. 1940-1950. 7" x 24". *Courtesy of Dave Beck.*

Canada Dry Hi-Spot tin sign. 7" x 24". *Courtesy of Dave Beck.*

Cheer Up double-sided tin sign, c. 1950s. 10″ x 12″. Courtesy of Dave Beck.

Tin Clem's Cola sign, c. 1950s. 18″ x 35″. Courtesy of Dave Beck.

Coleman's Ginger Ale tin sign, c. 1940s. The Mathews Co., Detroit, 18″ x 35″. Courtesy of Dave Beck.

Tin sign for Crush, c. 1950s. Scioto Sign Co., Kenyon, Ohio, 3.5" x 27". *Courtesy of Dave Beck.*

Crystal Club Beverages tin sign. Tal Soda Water Co., Scranton, Pennsylvania, 10" x 28". *Courtesy of Oliver's Auction Gallery.*

Porcelain enamel Dr. Pepper sign from the early 1940s. 10" x 24". *Courtesy of David Justice and Beth Fraser.*

Dee-Light tin sign, c. 1930s. Burdick Company Inc., New York, 18" x 6". *Courtesy of Gary Metz.*

Tall Dr. Pepper tin sign, c. 1930s. Robertson Steel & Iron Co., Springfield, Ohio, 54″ x 18″. *Courtesy of Gary Metz.*

Tin Dr. Pepper gas station sign with square blackboard, c. 1935. W. F. Robertson Steel & Iron Co., Springfield, Ohio. 38″ x 17″. *Courtesy of Gary Metz.*

Soda fountain sign for Dr. Pepper, c. 1940. Cardboard, 8.5″ x 11″. *Courtesy of Jay and Joan Millman.*

Tin Dr. Swett's Root Beer sign, c. 1920s. H.D. Beech Co.,
Coshocton, Ohio, 9″ x 24″. *Courtesy of Gary Metz.*

Dr. Wells Carbonated Beverage tin sign, c. 1940s. 3″ x 24″.
Courtesy of Dave Beck.

Five-O tin sign, late 1930s. 12″ x 24″. *Courtesy of Dave
Beck.*

Die-cut Hire's Root Beer stand-up cardboard sign, c. 1890. 9.5 x 6.5. *Courtesy of an anonymous collector.*

This great cowboy image is for Hartshorn's Root Beer Extract. Paper with lithography by Singer, Boston. *Courtesy of Oliver's Auction Gallery.*

Beveled edge Hire's sign, celluloid over tin, c. 1915. Manufactured by Permanent Advertising, Reading, Pennsylvania, 10" x 7". Haskell Coffin, artist. *Courtesy of Dennis and Gloria Healzer.*

June Kola tin sign, 1950s. Parker Metal, Baltimore, Maryland, 11.5″ x 23.5″. *Courtesy of Dave Beck.*

Round Howel's Root Beer sign,1950s. American Art Works, Inc., Coshocton, Ohio. 24″ in diameter. *Courtesy of Dave Beck.*

The pretty lady on this round tin sign invites us to join her for a Jersey-Creme. Made by the Charles W. Shonk Litho Co., Chicago, circa 1908. 12″ in diameter. *Courtesy of Herb and Elaine Aschendorf.*

Kayo tin sign and menu board, c. 1930s. 8″ x 13.5″. *Courtesy of Dave Beck.*

Lucky Sam soda, c. 1940s. Tin, 14″ x 30″, manufactured by the Vernon Co., Newton, Iowa. *Courtesy of Dave Beck.*

Tin sign for M & S Beverages, Flint, Michigan, c. 1930s. The Donaldson Art Sign Co., Covington, Kentucky. 18″ x 35″. *Courtesy of Dave Beck.*

Mavis Chocolate Drink sign, c. 1940s. Tin, 9.5″ x 13″, American Art Works, Inc., Coshocton, Ohio. *Courtesy of Gary Metz.*

Moxie sign, c. 1919-1920. Tin, 13.5″ x 20″. *Courtesy of Joe and Sue Ferriola.*

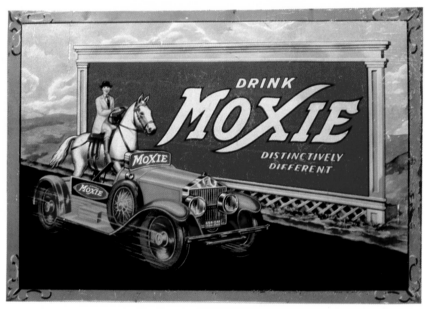

Composition Moxie, 35.5″ tall, 11″ in diameter. *Courtesy of Oliver's Auction Gallery.*

Tin Moxie sign, early 1930s. 13″ x 18.5″. *Courtesy of Joe and Sue Ferriola.*

Nesbitt's Orange tin sign, c. 1940s. 5″ x 13″. *Courtesy of Dave Beck.*

Nesbitt's Orange tin sign, c. 1960s. Stout Sign Co., St. Louis, 12″ x 30″. *Courtesy of Dave Beck.*

Nichol Kola tin sign, late 1930s. Parker Metal Co., Baltimore, 24″ x 8″. *Courtesy of Dave Beck.*

This cardboard Pepsi sign from the 1940s has seen considerable wear. 31″ x 24″ *Courtesy of Jay and Joan Millman.*

Norka Orange tin sign, Norka Beverage Co., Akron Ohio. 12″ x 24″. *Courtesy of Oliver's Auction Gallery.*

R-Pep Drink tin sign, 1930s. 18″ x 35″. *Courtesy of Dave Beck.*

Rainbow Beverages, Fladung Bottling Works, tin sign, 1940s. 12″ x 24″. *Courtesy of Dave Beck.*

Red Rock Cola tin sign, c. 1940s. 12″ x 24″. *Courtesy of Dave Beck.*

Royal Crown Cola tin sign, c. 1930s. Donaldson Art Sign Co., Covington, Kentucky, 30″ x 8″. *Courtesy of Dave Beck.*

Royal Crown Cola tin sign, 1930s.
12" x 29.75". *Courtesy of Dave Beck.*

Tin sign for Ski soda, 1960s. 12" x 32". *Courtesy of Dave Beck.*

Two-sided tin sign for Smile, c. 1930s. 10" x 12.5". *Courtesy of Dave Beck.*

Sun Crest sign, c. 1940s. Tin, 21" x 7.5". *Courtesy of Dave Beck.*

Smile tin sign, c. 1930s. Stout Sign Co., St. Louis, 2" x 10". *Courtesy of Dave Beck.*

Sun Crest sign, c. 1950s. Tin, 12″ x 29.5″. *Courtesy of Dave Beck.*

3V Cola tin sign. Press Sign Co., St. Louis. *Courtesy of Bob Thomas.*

Tower Root Beer tin sign, 13″ x 19″. Prospect Hill Bottling Co., Somerville, Massachusetts. *Courtesy of Oliver's Auction Gallery.*

Tin Whistle sign, 1930s. American Art Works, Coshocton, Ohio, 9″ x 28.5″. *Courtesy of Dave Beck.*

White Rock Girl litho in original mat and frame. 21″ x 16″. *Courtesy of Oliver's Auction Gallery.*

Triple AAA Root Beer sign, c. 1940s. Stout Sign Co., St. Louis, 44″ x 13″. *Courtesy of Dave Beck.*

White Rock Table Water tin sign, 10.5" in diameter. It has its original ornate gold frame. Shonk Litho, Chicago, 1881. *Courtesy of Oliver's Auction Gallery.*

Yuengling's Porter tin sign, c. 1940s-50s. National Sign Mfg. Co., Canisteo, New York, 9.5" x 28". *Courtesy of Dave Beck.*

COCA-COLA

Rare early Coca-Cola sign, embossed tin, 13.75" x 9.5". This nice sign has eight nail holes around the edge and one in the center. Charles Shonk Litho, Chicago, Illinois, No. C592. *Courtesy of Oliver's Auction Gallery.*

Beautiful Coca-Cola sign, copyrighted 1898. Enamel on paper by Wolf & Company, Philadelphia. 20" x 15.5". *Courtesy of Gary Metz.*

Coca-Cola festoon, 1922. This rare item is 39" long. *Courtesy of Oliver's Auction Gallery.*

Coca-Cola sign from a gas station with a chalkboard circle for the current gasoline prices, 1926. Tin, 14.5" x 24". *Courtesy of Gary Metz.*

Opposite page:

Top left: 1899 tin Coca-Cola sign, 18" x 26". One of two known, this beautiful sign depicts Hilda Clark, a famous opera singer.

Top right: 1910 Coca-Cola poster, 19" x 28", with a beautiful Gibson girl. The artist was B. Tichtman. Copyright, S.L. Whitten.

Center left: 1909 Coca-Cola tray in very nice condition. 16.5".

Center: 1905 Coca-Cola tray, 10.5" x 13".

Center right: Wonderful 1908 Coca-Cola calendar. The elegant lady sits in front of a Coca-Cola fountain.

Bottom left: 1922 Coca-Cola calendar with a full pad. There is a nice baseball scene in the background. Forbes Litho.

Bottom center: 1914 Betty Coca-Cola calendar.

Bottom right: Coke tray in outstanding condition. 13" x 10.75"; 1906 Coke change tray, very fine condition. *Courtesy of Oliver's Auction Gallery.*

Tin Coca-Cola sign with weathered wood frame. 66" x 26". *Courtesy of Oliver's Auction Gallery.*

Round 1933 embossed tin Coca-Cola sign, 20" in diameter. *Courtesy of Oliver's Auction Gallery.*

Tin Coca-Cola sign from a gas station with a chalkboard circle for the current gasoline prices, 1929. American Art Works Inc., Coshocton, Ohio, 20″ x 28″. *Courtesy of Gary Metz.*

Tin Coke sign, c. 1950s. 23″ x 23″. *Courtesy of Dave Beck.*

Two-sided porcelain enamel Coca-Cola fountainsign, dated 1940. 25″ x 26″. *Courtesy of David Justice and Beth Fraser.*

Coca-Cola tin sign. 60.5" x 27.5". *Courtesy of Oliver's Auction Gallery.*

1960s Coke sign, 12" x 32". *Courtesy of Dave Beck.*

Coca-Cola tin sign, c. 1940s. 12" x 24". *Courtesy of Dave Beck.*

Tin 1948 Coca-Cola sign, 32" x 14". American Art Works, Coshocton, 1949. *Courtesy of Oliver's Auction Gallery.*

BEER & ALE

Self-framing tin sign for the American Brewing Association's Pilsener beer. Kaufmann & Strauss Co., New York, 22.5" x 17". *Courtesy of Herbert Ramsey.*

Three masonite Coca-Cola record signs, 12" in diameter, 1950s.

Tin Budweiser sign, 8.5" x 13.5". American Art Sign, Coshocton, Ohio. *Courtesy of Jay and Joan Millman.*

Budweiser-Faust leaded glass window from the Savoy Hotel in St. Louis, c. 1890. 31" x 47". *Courtesy of Oliver's Auction Gallery.*

Self-framing tin Budweiser sign, c. 1890-1900. 26" x 18". *Courtesy of Phil Perdue.*

Round tin Budweiser sign, c. 1905-1910. 10" in diameter. *Courtesy of Jay and Joan Millman.*

Carling's Ale sign, c. 1940s, Lawson Wood, artist. Donaldson Art Sign Co., Covington, Kentucky. 12″ x 18″. *Courtesy of Dave Beck.*

Porcelain enamel corner sign for Brazil Beer, c. 1910. Burdick Enamel & Belair Stamping Co., Baltimore, Maryland. 20″ x 11.5″. DJ

Tin Chief Oshkosh Beer sign, late 1920s. American Art Works, Coshocton, Ohio. 13.5″ x 18″. *Courtesy of David Justice and Beth Fraser.*

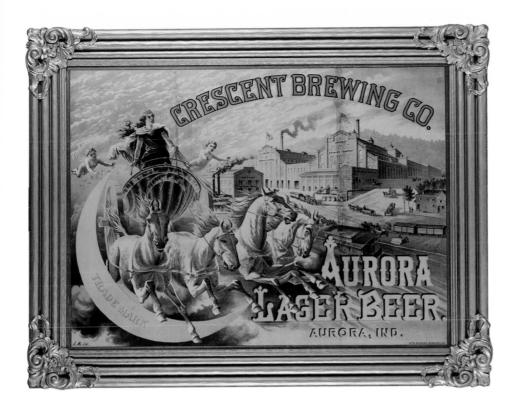

Strong images and graphics mark this Crescent Brewing Company paper sign, c. 1885. Marked "E.M. Litho" and "Wm. B. Burford, Indianapolis, Ind." 29.5″ x 37″. *Courtesy of The Hug Collection.*

Foss-Schneider Brewing Co. / Queen City Brewery, Cincinnati, paper sign, c. 1883. Krebs Litho, Cincinnati, 28.5″ x 22″. *Courtesy of The Hug Collection.*

Embossed, die-cut cardboard calendar for Grand Rapids Brewing Co., 1906. To prove the healthy benefits of their brew, the girl is reading an endorsement in "Dr. Hall's Health Hints, Published by U.S. Health Ass'n." 14.5″ x 10″. *Courtesy of Harold and Elsie Edmondson.*

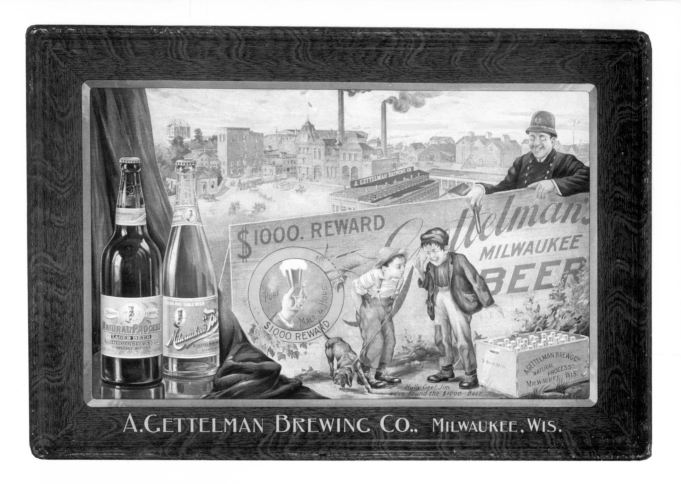

A. GETTELMAN BREWING CO., MILWAUKEE, WIS.

Gettelman Brewing Co., self-framing tin sign. A beautiful and rare sign from Meek Litho, Coshocton, Ohio. *Courtesy of Oliver's Auction Gallery.*

Harvard Ale lighted glass and metal sign, 22 inches in diameter. *Courtesy of Oliver's Auction Gallery.*

Harvard Beer tin sign is in near mint condition with wonderful graphics. Meek Litho, Coshocton, Ohio, 27″ x 35″. *Courtesy of Oliver's Auction Gallery.*

Tin sign with a wonderful humorous scene from the brewery, painted by Wiener. Hoster Brewery, Columbus, Ohio, 17.5" x 21.5". *Courtesy of Oliver's Auction Gallery.*

Krueger Beer and Ale tin on cardboard sign, c. 1930s. Philadelphia Badge Co., Philadelphia, Pennsylvania. *Courtesy of Herb and Elaine Aschendorf.*

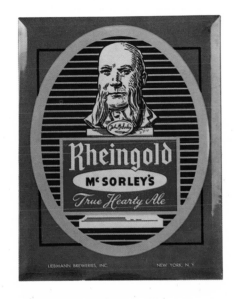

McSorley's Rheingold Ale sign, coated tin, c. 1938-1940. Permanent Sign & Display Co., Reading, Pennsylvania, 9" x 7". *Courtesy of Jay and Joan Millman.*

Opposite page:
Wonderful tin sign for Moerleins Beer. 19.5″ x 26″. *Courtesy of Oliver's Auction Gallery.*

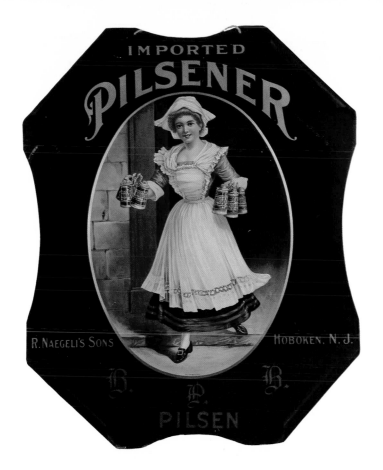

R. Naegell's Sons rolled tin sign for Pilsner Beer. The Meek Co., Coshocton, Ohio, 15.5″ x 21.5″. *Courtesy of Oliver's Auction Gallery.*

Reverse glass Narragansett Lager Beer sign. This is the only known example of a beautiful sign. Hope Manufacturing Co., 35″ x 22.5″. *Courtesy of Oliver's Auction Gallery.*

Very unusual J.F. Oertel Brewery saddle sign, leather and brass. 21.5″ x 17.5″ *Courtesy of Mike and Doris Brown.*

Fred. Opperman Jr. sign, Turtle Bay Brewery, New York. This brewery was probably in business for only 4 or 5 years. 18″ x 6.75″. *Courtesy of the House of Stewart.*

Old Craft Brew lithograph on canvas, 1934. A nice fantasy image for the Leisen & Henes Brewing Co., Menominee, Michigan. 21.5″ x 28.5″. *Courtesy of Betty Blair.*

Pabst Blue Ribbon Beer tin sign, c. 1920s. Marked "Form MA122B," 11.5" x 18". *Courtesy of Dave Beck.*

R & H Beer tin sign, c. 1930s. American Art Sign Co., Coshocton, Ohio, 9" x 13". *Courtesy of Jay and Joan Millman.*

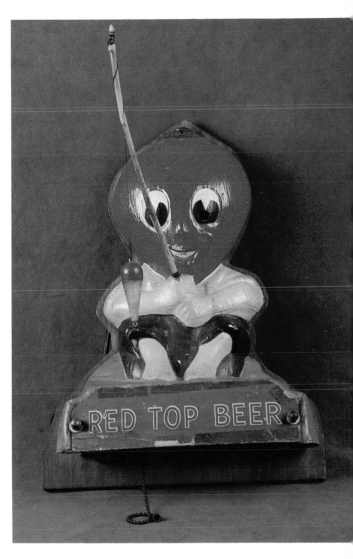

Red Top Beer and Ale moving sign, c. 1940s. Papier mâche with a wood back and a light inside. 15" x 10.5" x 4.5". *Courtesy of Bob Thomas.*

Ram's Head Ale tin sign, c. 1930s. Philadelphia Badge Co., Inc. Philadelphia, 9" in diameter. *Courtesy of Jay and Joan Millman.*

Ruppert's Beer tin sign, c. 1930s. 9" x 13.5". *Courtesy of Jay and Joan Millman.*

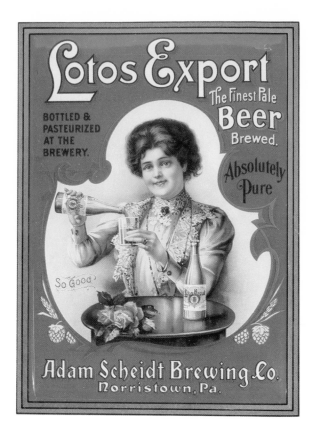

Celluloid sign for the Adam Scheidt Brewing Company's Lotos Export. Wonderful color. 10" x 14". *Courtesy of Oliver's Auction Gallery.*

Schlitz tin sign, c. 1905-1910. Chas. W. Shonk, Chicago, 28.5" x 22". *Courtesy of Jay and Joan Millman.*

Embossed paper sign for the Ste. Genevieve Brewing and Lighting Association, Ste. Genevieve, Missouri, c. 1910-1919. 17.5" x 11". *Courtesy of Fil and Robbie Graf.*

Silver Spring Ale tin sign, c. 1950s. 9″ x 19.5″. *Courtesy of Dave Beck.*

The subject of this self-framing tin sign does not quite suit modern sensibilities. The work however is beautiful. Standard Brewing Co., of Mankato, Minnesota. On the reverse is a paper describing the new brewery at Mankato and the story of the execution of 38 Sioux under President Lincoln's order for the crime of killing white "children." Interestingly the history contains a prohibition against alcoholic beverages preceding the hanging. This did not seem to stop the officers on the porch from thoroughly enjoying the occasion. Tin, 26″ x 18″. *Courtesy of Oliver's Auction Gallery.*

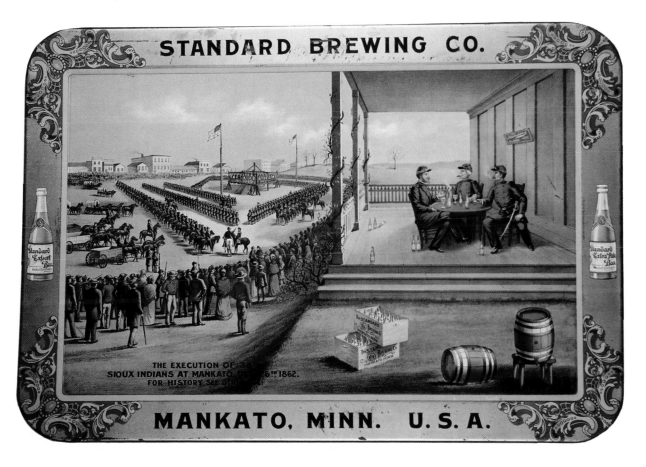

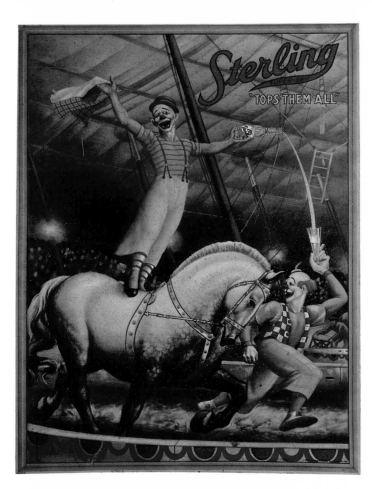

Stroh's plastic on tin sign, late 1940s. Prismatic Sign by Bastian Bros., Rochester, New York, 15″ x 6″. *Courtesy of Jay and Joan Millman.*

Nice Columbian Extra Pale Bottled Beer embossed tin sign, the Tennessee Brewing Co., Memphis. H.D. Beach Co., Coshocton, Ohio, 13.5″ x 9.75″. *Courtesy of Oliver's Auction Gallery.*

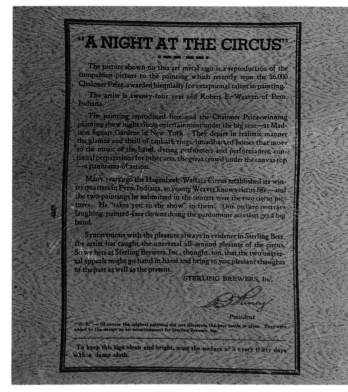

Tin sign for Sterling beer, dated 1938. The artist is Robert E. Weaver of Peru, Indiana. The painting originally won the $6000 Chalomer Prize. The beer and glass were added for the advertisement. 27″ x 21″. *Courtesy of Oliver's Auction Gallery.*

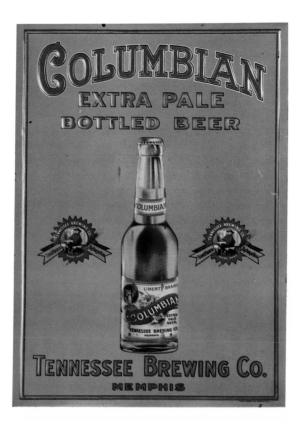

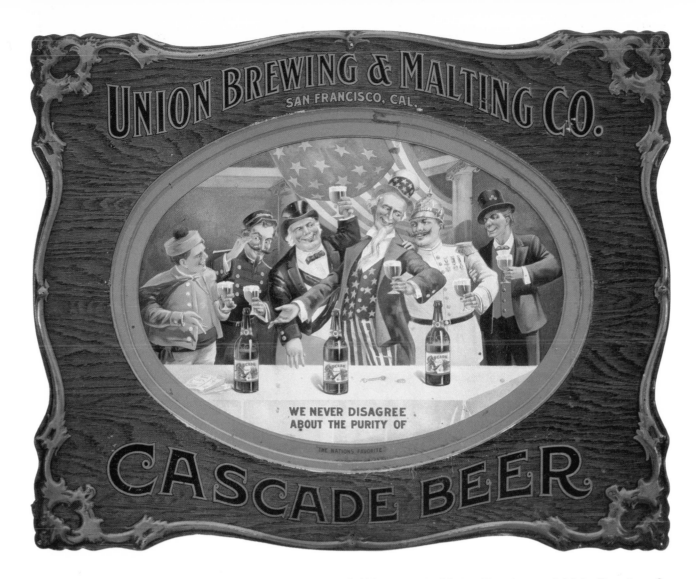

Self-framing tin Union Brewing and Malt Co. sign, San Francisco. This Cascade Beer sign features Uncle Sam and his international buddies. 21" x 15.5". *Courtesy of Oliver's Auction Gallery.*

Tin West End Brewery sign, c. 1904. 24.5" x 20.5". *Courtesy of Dick and Katie Bucht.*

WHISKEY AND OTHER SPIRITS

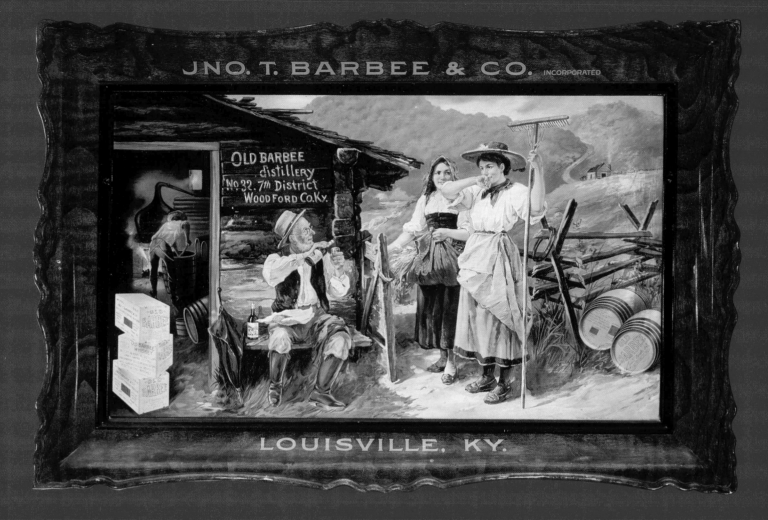

Tin Barbee Whiskey self-framing sign. 31″ x 19″. *Courtesy of Oliver's Auction Gallery.*

Rolled tin sign for Bellmore Whiskey, Bernard Fischer, Inc., c. 1910-1911. Chas. W. Shonk Co., Chicago. 14″ x 14″. *Courtesy of Joe and Sue Ferriola.*

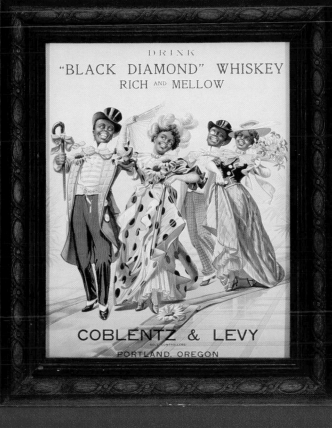

Coblentz and Levy, Portland, Oregon paper sign for Black Diamond Whiskey. Image size 14" x 18.5". *Courtesy of Oliver's Auction Gallery.*

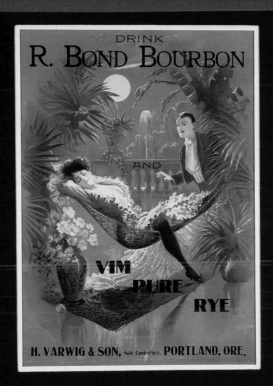

The beautiful lady in an outrageous pose and the delightfully surprised gentleman make an enchanted advertisement for R. Bond Bourbon and Vim Pure Rye. H. Varwig and Son, Portland Oregon. 14" x 21". *Courtesy of Oliver's Auction Gallery.*

Paper sign for Block, Franck, & Co., c. 1910. Gast Art Litho, St. Louis, 22" x 16.5". *Courtesy of Mike and Doris Brown.*

Paper sign for the L. Dryfoos Co., sole distributors of Bleak House, Rosemont, and Old Barbee Whiskey, Seattle, Washington, c. 1905. The image measures 19.5" x 15.5". *Courtesy of The Hug Collection.*

Tin sign for Holoway's London Dry Gin, c. 1920s. 14″ x 11.5″. *Courtesy of Mike and Doris Brown.*

Die-cut tin whiskey sign, Friedman-Keifer & Co. American Art Works, Coshocton, Ohio, 19″ x 6″. *Courtesy of Oliver's Auction Gallery.*

Tin Green River Whiskey sign in its original frame, 1899. Chas. Shonk Litho, Chicago, Illinois, 33″ x 23″. *Courtesy of Oliver's Auction Gallery.*

"The Temptation of St. Anthony." Rolled tin sign for Paul Jones Whiskey, c. 1900. 20" x 13.5. *Courtesy of R.A.G. Time.*

Rolled tin sign for Paul Jones Pure Gin, c. 1900-1905, Paul Jones and Company, Louisville, Kentucky. The sign was manufactured by the Meek Co., Coshocton, Ohio, 19.5" x 14". *Courtesy of Kim and Mary Kokles.*

Litho on glass sign for the Wm. Drueke Company's Lakeside Club Bouquet Whiskey. 26" x 30" including frame. *Courtesy of Gary Metz.*

Paper on cardboard Montreal Malt Rye sign, c. 1910-1915. Donaldson Art Sign Co., Covington, Kentucky. 18″ x 24″. *Courtesy of Mike and Doris Brown.*

Very early lithographed tin sign for O.F.C. whiskey, c. 1890s. Sentivi & Green, 17″ x 12″. *Courtesy of Jay and Joan Millman.*

O.F.C. Rye paper sign: "A Stag Party" by C. Everett Johnson. 30″ x 21″. *Courtesy of The Olde Mercantile Store.*

O.F.C. Whiskey embossed tin sign in original frame. 27″ x 19″. *Courtesy of Oliver's Auction Gallery.*

Pride of Kentucky Whiskey paper sign, Wiedeman Fries & Co., Cleveland, Ohio, 1896. Litho by Louis Wagner Co., New York. Original gold leaf wooden carved frame. *Courtesy of Oliver's Auction Gallery.*

Reversed painted on glass Stoll & Company sign, with a beautiful rendition of the company's plant, dated 1901. The Tuchfarber Co., Cincinnati, Ohio, 20″ x 28″. The frame is original. *Courtesy of Mike and Doris Brown.*

Reverse painted on glass sign for Sylvan Grove Whiskey, from the Fleischmann Co. 30" x 20". *Courtesy of Gary Metz.*

Cardboard sign for Wolfe's Schnapps, c. 1910. 21.5" x 27.5". *Courtesy of Hitchner-Morrison.*

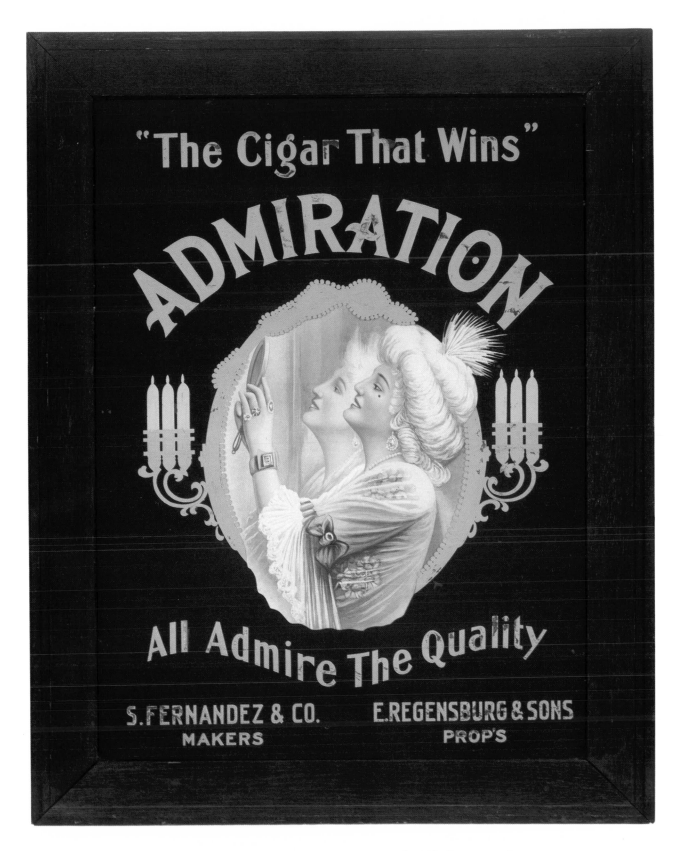

Reverse glass Admiration Cigar sign. 17" x 23". *Courtesy of Oliver's Auction Gallery.*

Superb Allen & Ginter paper sign showing a set of cigarette cards, as well as a buffalo and Indian scene. Lindner, Eddy, and Clauss Litho, New York, 29″ x 20″. *Courtesy of Oliver's Auction Gallery.*

Early paper Bengal Cheroots sign, c. 1885. Isaac Friedenwald Litho, Baltimore, Maryland. 23.5″ x 15.5″. *Courtesy of the Kit Barry Collection.*

Tin Bloodhound Chew sign, c. 1950s. 18″ x 27.5″ *Courtesy of Dave Beck.*

Paper sign for Bloomer Club Cigar. 20.5″ x 15″. *Courtesy of Oliver's Auction Gallery.*

Another Buchanan & Lyall paper poster, part of the "Firemen, Past and Present" series, 1895. Original frame. *Courtesy of Oliver's Auction Gallery.*

Paper poster for Buchanan & Lyall's Tobacco. H.A. Thomas & Wylie Litho Co., New York, 21″ x 27″. *Courtesy of Oliver's Auction Gallery.*

Buchanan and Lyall's Tobacco paper sign, 28″ x 21″. H.A. Thomas and Wylie Litho, 1895. *Courtesy of Oliver's Auction Gallery.*

Tin Devilish Good Cigar sign. Sentenne & Green, New York, 10″ x 13.5″. *Courtesy of Oliver's Auction Gallery.*

Duke's Mixture tin sign. 11″ x 8″. *Courtesy of Gary Metz.*

Celluloid sign for "Ditto" Cigar, Ruhe Bros. Co., Mfgrs, c. 1910-1919. The 12″ x 8″ sign is by Whitehead & Hoag, Newark, New Jersey and made of "Crystaloid," a product patented in May, 1906. *Courtesy of Joe and Sue Ferriola.*

Small Duke's Mixture porcelain enamel sign. Liggett & Myers Tobacco Co., 8.5" x 4.25". *Courtesy of Jay and Joan Millman.*

Three dimensional cardboard Fatima Cigars counter display, c. 1920s. 22" x 30" x 7". *Courtesy of Dick and Katie Bucht.*

A cozy scene in this paper poster for General Cigar Co., National Brands, 34" x 23". *Courtesy of Dave Beck.*

Opposite page, top right:
General Cigar Co., National Brands paper poster, 34.5" x 23.5". *Courtesy of Dave Beck.*

Opposite page, bottom left:
Nice paper poster for General Cigar Co. National Brands products. 35.5" x 24.5", marked Series No. 156. *Courtesy of Bill Powell, American Arts.*

Opposite page, top right:
Oil cloth sign for Hammer Cigars, c. 1910. Ronemous & Co., Baltimore, Maryland, 14" x 9". *Courtesy of Dennis and Gloria Healzer.*

Opposite page, bottom right:
Paper sign in original frame for Helmar Turkish Cigarettes, c. 1920s. 31" x 20". *Courtesy of Joe and Sue Ferriola.*

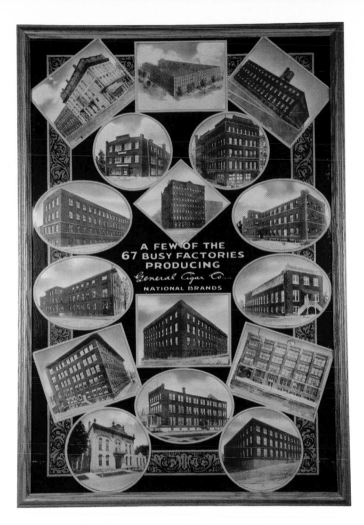

A FEW OF THE
67 BUSY FACTORIES
PRODUCING
General Cigar Co.
NATIONAL BRANDS

'IT KEEPS A NOCKEN'
· CIGARS ·
THE HAMMER
COSTS 5¢

On your vacation *enjoy*
your favorite well known brand
Rob.t Burns
White Owl
Wm. Penn
"Laddies"

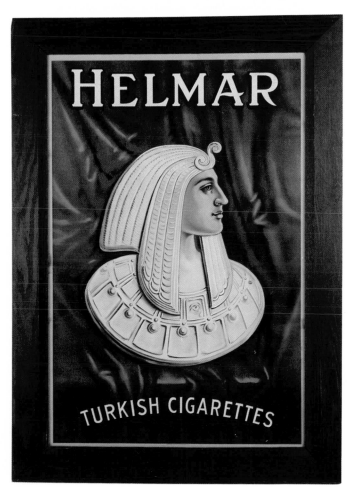

HELMAR

TURKISH CIGARETTES

Hoffman House Bouquet Cigars paper sign, copyright 1900. Gray Litho, 10.5″ x 13.5″ image size. *Courtesy of Oliver's Auction Gallery.*

Paper sign with outstanding color for Home Run Cigarettes, late 19th century. 17.5″ x 12″. Only known example. *Courtesy of Oliver's Auction Gallery.*

Tin Kool cigarettes sign, c. 1940s-50s. 12″ x 30″. *Courtesy of Dave Beck.*

Tin Kool cigarettes sign, c. 1960s-70s. 12" x 30". *Courtesy of Dave Beck.*

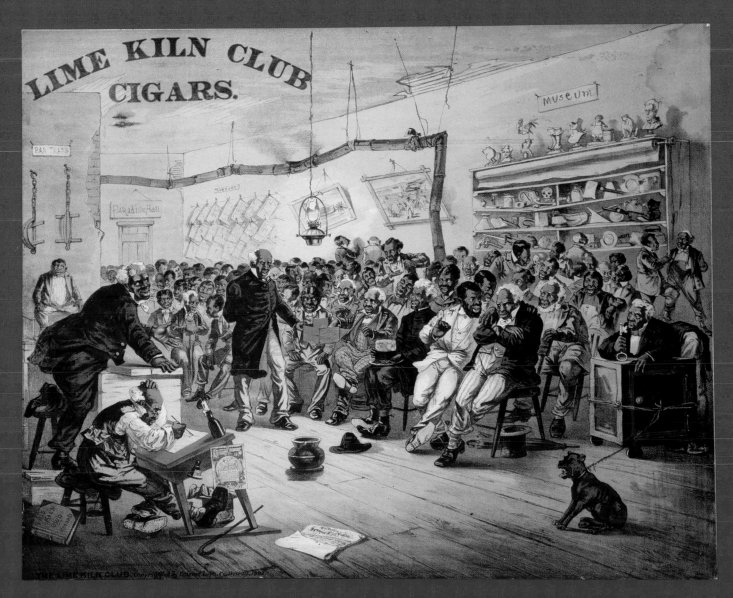

Limekiln Club Cigars poster, 1882. Litho on paper laid down on canvas, 30.5" x 24". *Courtesy of Oliver's Auction Gallery.*

Paper sign for P. Lorillard Tobacco depicting Lillian Russell in five costumes. A rare sign from Giles Litho, New York, 26″ x 41″. *Courtesy of Oliver's Auction Gallery.*

Die-cut cardboard stand-up sign for Mail Pouch Tobacco, c. 1930s. *Courtesy of Gary Metz.*

Paper Lucky Strike sign, c. 1940s. 35″ x 27″. *Courtesy of Gary Metz.*

Porcelain enamel MacDonald's Cut Golden Bar, c. 1900. 30″ x 22″. *Courtesy of David Justice and Beth Fraser.*

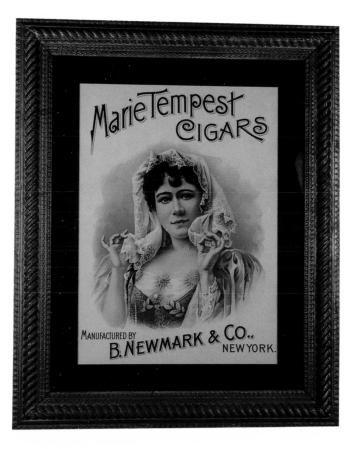

Marie Tempest Cigars, B. Newmark & Co., New York. 31.5″ x 25.5″ with frame. *Courtesy of Joe and Sue Ferriola.*

Murad self-framing tin sign, c. 1910. 39″ x 28″. *Courtesy of Harold and Elsie Edmondson.*

Mecca Cigarettes paper sign in original frame. American Tobacco Co., T. Earl Christy, artist. 18″ x 9.5″. *Courtesy of Oliver's Auction Gallery.*

Model Smoking Tobacco, c. 1940s. 11.5 x 35″. *Courtesy of an anonymous collector.*

Ink-fired porcelain enamel Murad sign. The image on this two-sided sign was applied by applying a wet decal before sending it through the kiln. 20″ x 12″, circa 1905. *Courtesy of David Justice and Beth Fraser.*

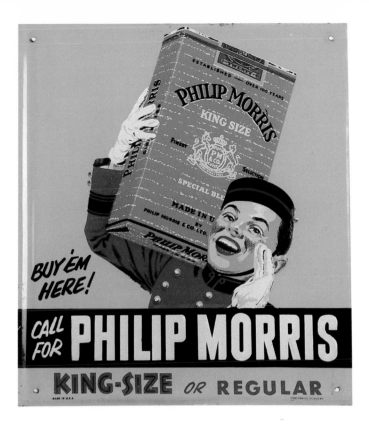

Philip Morris tin sign, c. 1940s. Stout Sign Co., St. Louis, 14″ x 12″. *Courtesy of Gary Metz.*

Pay Car Scrap slightly embossed tin sign. 18″ x 13.75″. *Courtesy of Oliver's Auction Gallery.*

Perfection Cigarettes paper sign in original wood frame, c. 1910-1920. 27″ x 20.5″ *Courtesy of Bygones By Blake.*

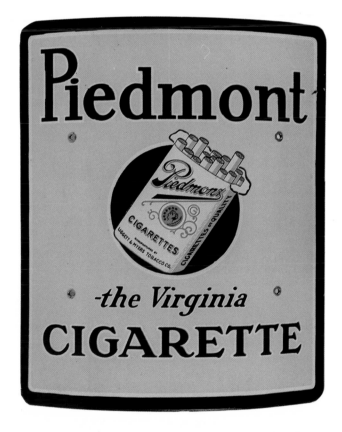

Porcelain enamel curved corner sign for Piedmont Cigarettes, c. 1910-1920. 16″ x 13″. *Courtesy of Gary Metz.*

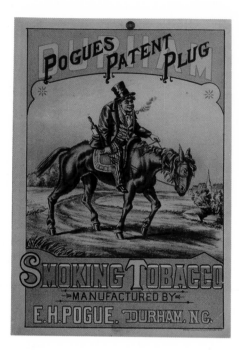

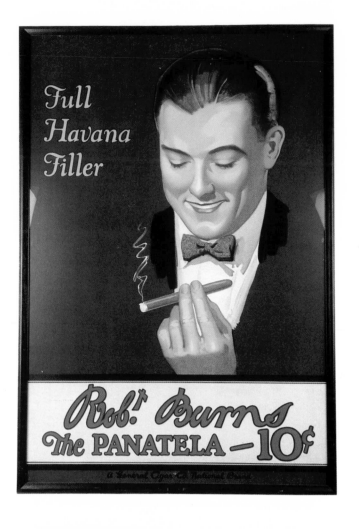

San Felice Cigars porcelain enamel sign, c. 1920s. 13″ x
38.5″. *Courtesy of Joe and Sue Ferriola.*

Humorous poster for Seal of North Carolina Cut Plug, c.
1880-1890. Signed: Lucas. 17″ x 12″ *Courtesy of John
Kemler with Dale Kemler.*

Opposite page, top left:
Nice early cardboard hanging sign for Pogue's Patent Plug,
Durham, North Carolina, c. 1880s. Empire Litho & Eng.,
249 Pearl St., New York, 10″ x 7″. *Courtesy of Gary Metz.*
Opposite page, bottom left:
Rob't Burns Cigar paper poster. *Courtesy of Dave Beck.*
Opposite page, top right:
Rob't Burns Cigar poster, 34″ x 23″. *Courtesy of Dave
Beck.*
Opposite page, bottom right:
Tin Royal Banner Cigar sign, Banner Cigar Mfg. Co.,
Detroit, c. 1895. Meek Co., Coshocton, Ohio, 24″ x 18″.
Courtesy of The Olde Mercantile Store.

Who could refuse a cigar from this beautiful lady? Stickney's
New Tariff Cigar, c. 1905-1910. Signed by the artist but
illegible (DAC?). 30″ x 21″. *Courtesy of Fil and Robbie Graf.*

Heavy paper hanging sign for Three Feathers tobacco. One side depicts the tin and the other the pack. 16″ in diameter. *Courtesy of Joe and Sue Ferriola.*

Tomahawk Plug heavy cardboard die-cut sign, c. 1870-1880. P. Lorillard's Co., Jersey City, New Jersey, 35″ x 17″. *Courtesy of The Olde Mercantile Store.*

Three Kings Vanity Fair Cigarettes, W.S. Kimball, 1882. Major and Knapp Litho Co., 29″ x 23″. *Courtesy of Oliver's Auction Gallery.*

Van Dyck Cigar poster, paper, 35″ x 23.5″. *Courtesy of Dave Beck.*

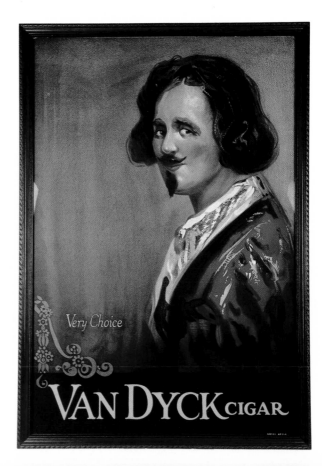

Tin sign for WDC Special Pipes, 13.5″ x 9.5″. *Courtesy of Joe and Sue Ferriola.*

Wm. Penn poster, signed W.E.R., 36″ x 24.5″ with frame. *Courtesy of Bill Powell, American Arts.*

Embossed, die-cut signs of heavy cardboard for "War Eagle" Cheroots, c. 1898. One features U.S. Navy heroes while the other honors the heroes of the army. 14.5" x 10.5". *Courtesy of John Kemler.*

REMEDIES AND CURES

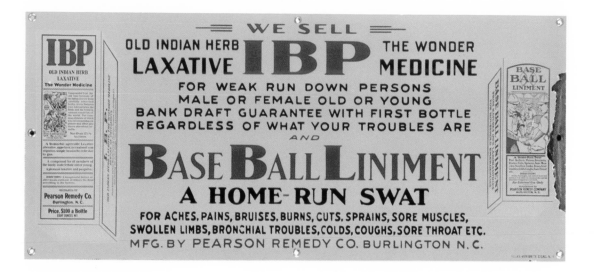

Porcelain enamel sign for Base Ball Liniment, c. 1910. Nelke-Veribrite Signs, New York, 12" x 30". *Courtesy of Gary Metz.*

Aluminum Braem's Bitters sign, manufactured by Aluminum Sign Co., Kewaunee, Wisconsin. 13.5" x 7". *Courtesy of Dave Beck.*

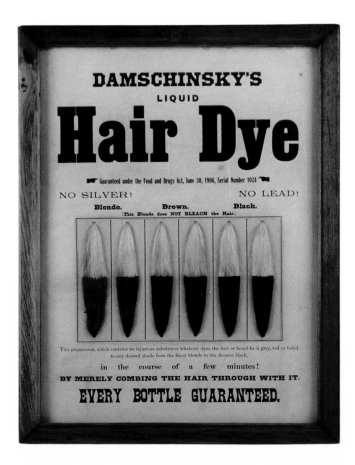

Damschinsky's Liquid Hair Dye paper poster with samples, c. 1906-1910. 19" x 14". *Courtesy of Joe and Sue Ferriola.*

Dr. D. Jayne's Expectorant, paper roll-down signs with metal strips at each end. One depicts Washington, the other Jefferson. Both are 28″ x 13.5″. *Courtesy of Oliver's Auction Gallery.*

Tin sign for Dr. Morse Indian Root Pills, c. 1900. 10.5″ x 14″ and manufactured by the MacDonald Mfg. Co., To[ronto?] *Courtesy of the House of Stewart.*

Dr. Pierce's Anuric sign, paper, 45″ x 7.5″. *Dave Lowenthal, Hog Wild Antiques.*

Paper sign for Dr. Pierce's Anuric Tablets. Hayes Litho Co., Buffalo, New York, 7.75″ x 22″. *Dave Lowenthal, Hog Wild Antiques.*

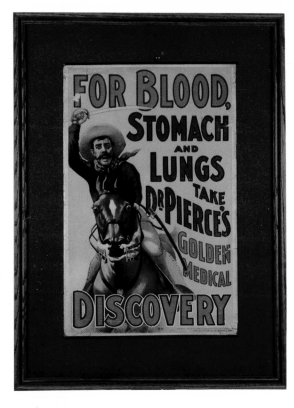

Aluminum sign for Garrison's Celery and Iron Brew, c. 1930s. 5″ x 7″. *Courtesy of Joe and Sue Ferriola.*

Dr. Pierce's Golden Medical Discovery sign. Roll-down canvas-like signs with metal strips on each end, 21.5″ x 14″. *Courtesy of Gary Metz.*

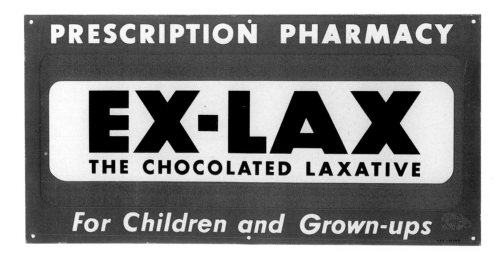

Tin Ex-Lax sign, c. 1940s. 12″ x 23.5″. *Courtesy of Dave Beck.*

Large paper sign for Owen's Pink Mixture, c. 1890-1900. 55″ x 42.5″. *Courtesy of John Kemler.*

Satin Skin Powder & Skin Cream paper sign, 41.5 x 27.5. Copyright 1903 by Albert F. Wood, M'F'R, The Satin Toilet Specialties, Detroit. *Courtesy of Oliver's Auction Gallery.*

Sanatogan Tonic Wine tin sign, c. 1920s-30s. 11″ x 8″. *Courtesy of Marcia and Bob Weissman.*

Cardboard sign for United States Medicine Co., dated 1884. Printed by Hatch Litho Co., New York, 15″ x 12″ *Courtesy of an anonymous collector.*

Sign for Buerger's Garden Flower fragrance, c. 1920s. 10" x 10". *Courtesy of Gary Metz.*

Paper sign for Colgate's talc. 30.5" x 20.5". *Courtesy of Joe and Sue Ferriola.*

Poster for B. T. Babbits Soap and Soap Powder, dated 1895. Donaldson Bros., New York, 28" x 14". *Courtesy of Gary Metz.*

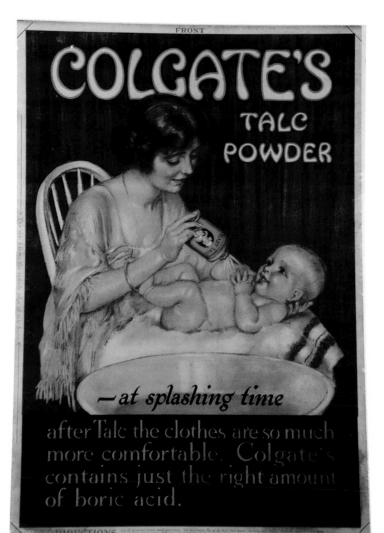

Paper sign for Empire Soap Co., dated 1887. Compton Litho Co., St. Louis, 26.5″ x 19″ framed. *Courtesy of Oliver's Auction Gallery.*

Paper sign for Colgate's talc. 30.5″ x 20.5″. *Courtesy of Joe and Sue Ferriola.*

Gold Dust cardboard sign. 10″ x 26″. *Courtesy of Frank's Antiques.*

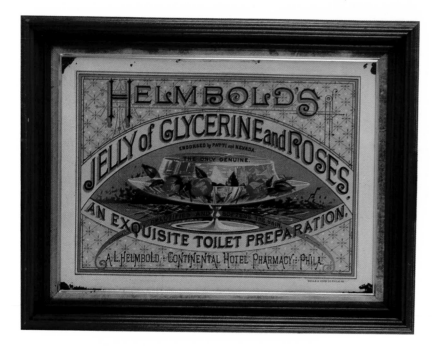

Early tin sign for Helmbold's Jelly of Glycerine and Roses, c. 1880s, a product of A.L. Helmbold Continental Hotel Pharmacy, Philadelphia. Wells & Hope Co., Philadelphia, Pennsylvania, 12" x 16". *Courtesy of Gary Metz.*

Very early tin sign for Hoyt's Cologne, Lowell, Massachusetts, c. 1880s. 14.75" x 23". *Courtesy of Oliver's Auction Gallery.*

Five framed Sapolio signs around the theme of "The Spotless Town." Paper, 10.5" x 20.5". *Courtesy of Oliver's Auction Gallery.*

Porcelain enamel Witch Soap sign, c. 1900-1910. British, 23" x 35". *Courtesy of Gary Metz.*

CLOTHING

Beacon Shoe tin sign, c. 1920s. 9.5" x 28". *Courtesy of an anonymous collector.*

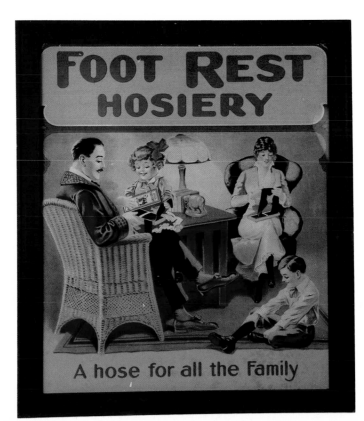

Die-cut Foot Rest Hosiery cardboard sign. U.S. Litho Co., Cincinnati & New York, 32" x 16.5". *Courtesy of Bill Powell, American Arts.*

Foot Rest Hosiery paper poster. U.S. Litho Co., Cincinnati & New York, 23.5" x 19.5". *Courtesy of Bill Powell, American Arts.*

R & G Corsets wrought iron and porcelain enamel sign, c. 1890s. Made by the Imperial Co., New York, the round portion is 10″ in diameter. *Courtesy of David Justice and Beth Fraser.*

J & P Coats paper sign. 30.5″ x 14.5″. *Courtesy of Bill Powell, American Arts.*

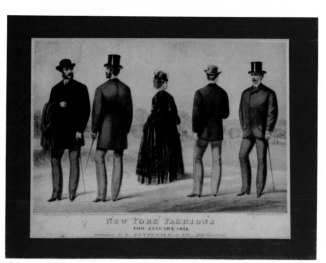

New York Fashion poster, dated 1870. Hatch & Co., New York, 11.5″ x 14″. *Courtesy of an anonymous collector.*

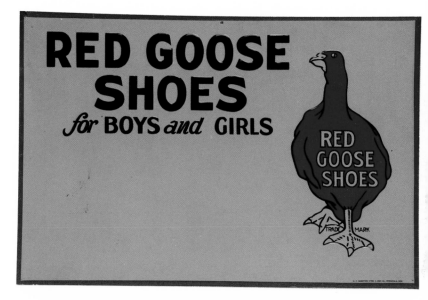

Red Goose Shoes tin sign, 13″ x 9″. W.P. Robertson Steel & Iron Co., Springfield, Ohio.

Red Goose Shoes porcelain enamel sign, early 1930s. 36" x 29.5". *Courtesy of David Justice and Beth Fraser.*

Card Board sign for Swim-Kaps, c. 1920s. 15" x 10.5". *Courtesy of Herb and Elaine Aschendorf.*

Sweet, Orr & Co's Overalls corner sign, 1904. Porcelain enamel, 14" x 18". *Courtesy of David Justice and Beth Fraser.*

Paper Walk-Over Shoes sign, c. 1920s. Signed by the artist R. Ford Harper. 30.5" x 11.5". *Courtesy of Joe and Sue Ferriola.*

Artist's proof for a poster for the Walley Cuff Holder, the H. H. Walley Co., North Adams, Massachusetts. Marked on the back: "H. H. Walley; March 29, '04, April 16, '04". 18.5" x 14.5". *Courtesy of Joe and Sue Ferriola.*

FARM SUPPLIES AND EQUIPMENT

A nice paper sign for the Auburn Wagon Co., Auburn, New York. 21.5" x 27.5". *Courtesy of Oliver's Auction Gallery.*

Embossed tin sign for the Aultman & Taylor Machinery Co., Mansfield, Ohio. The Meek Co., Coshocton, Ohio, 19.5" x 13.75". *Courtesy of Oliver's Auction Gallery.*

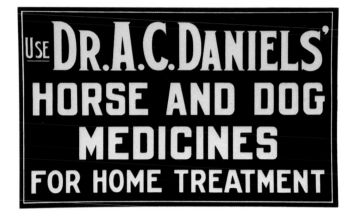

Embossed tin sign for Dr. A.C. Daniels Horse and Dog Medicines. 28" x 17.5". *Courtesy of Oliver's Auction Gallery.*

Left: Crossman Brothers seed poster, 1887. J. Ottman Litho, 19" x 24". Right: Woolson Spice poster, 19th century. Gast Litho, 22" x 32". *Courtesy of Oliver's Auction Gallery.*

What Rudolph Valentino has to do with Deering Giant Mowers or Light Reapers is unclear, but here he is on this interesting paper sign, c 1920s. 25" x 19". *Courtesy of Fil and Robbie Graf.*

De Laval tin sign in mint condition, with original marked frame. 19″ x 25″. *Courtesy of Oliver's Auction Gallery.*

Marathon Ethyl porcelain enamel sign, early 1930s. 30″ in diameter. *Courtesy of Frank's Antiques.*

Round Donald Duck RPM Motor Oil tin sign. Walt Disney Productions, 1940. 23.5″ in diameter. *Courtesy of Oliver's Auction Gallery.*

"Power Plus" gasoline two-sided porcelain enamel sign, 1930s. 24″ in diameter. *Courtesy of David Justice and Beth Fraser.*

Red Crown Gasoline porcelain enamel sign that would have been used on the old clear gas pump, c. 1915. 16″ in diameter. *Courtesy of David Justice and Beth Fraser.*

Left:
Tin sign for Reo Motor Cars, c. 1920s. 10″ x 27.75″. *Courtesy of Dave Beck.*
Center right:
Round Mickey Mouse Standard Oil tin sign. Walt Disney Productions, 1940. 23.5″ in diameter. *Courtesy of Oliver's Auction Gallery.*
Bottom right:
Twin City Garage Association tin sign, c. 1940s. 28″ x 16″. *Courtesy of Dave Beck.*

Shell-Penn Motor Oil porcelain enamel sign, late 1930s. 30″ x 29″. *Courtesy of David Justice and Beth Fraser.*

Porcelain enamel sign for Socony Parabase Motor Oil, late 1920s. 6″ x 9″. *Courtesy of David Justice and Beth Fraser.*

INSURANCE COMPANIES

Niagara Fire Insurance Company, New York. Reverse painted glass sign, 12.5″ x 16.5″, c. 1920s. *Courtesy of Jay and Joan Millman.*

Fireman's Fund Insurance Company, San Francisco. Self-framing tin sign, 30″ x 22″. *Courtesy of Oliver's Auction Gallery.*

Germania Life Insurance Company, New York. Framed paper poster, 29″ x 22.5″. Printed by Mayer, Merkel & Ottmann Litho. *Courtesy of Oliver's Auction Gallery.*

Providence Washington Insurance Company, Providence, Rhode Island. Paper sign, 23.5″ x 17.25″. *Courtesy of Oliver's Auction Gallery.*

Shawnee Fire Insurance Co., Topeka, Kansas. Porcelain enamel sign, 12″ x 18″. *Courtesy of David Justice and Beth Fraser.*

MISCELLANEOUS SIGNS AND POSTERS

Cristiani Bros. Circus paper poster, copyright 1958 by F. D. Freeland. 21.5″ x 27.5″. *Courtesy of Oliver's Auction Gallery.*

World War One poster issued by the Publication Section of the Emergency Fleet Corporation, Philadelphia and the U.S. Shipping Board. Forbes Litho, Boston, 60″ x 40″. *Courtesy of Oliver's Auction Gallery.*

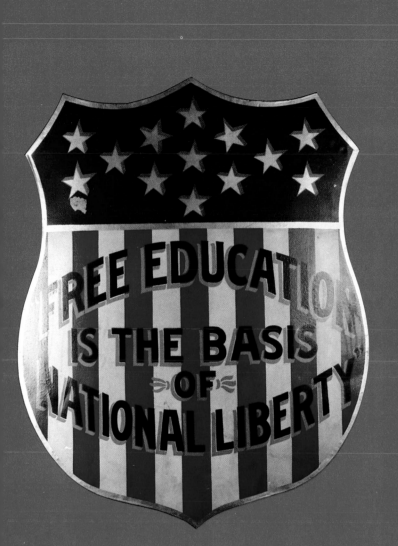

Advertising shield promoting *Free Education*. 33.5" x 28". Litho on steel. *Courtesy of Oliver's Auction Gallery.*

EM-GE Alarm Pistols porcelain enamel sign from the mid-1920s. 122" x 8". *Courtesy of David Justice and Beth Fraser.*

The New Great Syndicate Shows and Paris Hippodrome early paper poster glued to barn board. Russell and Morgan Factories Printing, Cincinnati, 39" x 26". *Courtesy of Oliver's Auction Gallery.*

Alligator Belt Lacing stand-up tin sign. American Can Co., Maywood, Illinois, 9" x 13". *Courtesy of Dave Beck.*

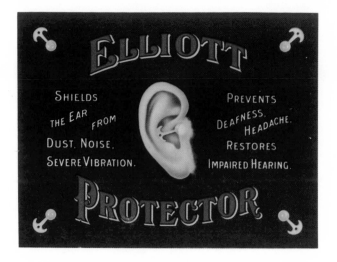

"Crystaloid" sign for Elliott Ear Protectors, c. 1910. The Whitehead & Hoag Co., Newark, New Jersey, 7.5" x 9.5". *Courtesy of Marcia and Bob Weissman.*

Atkins Saw company steel cased reversed painted glass sign which is lighted from the back, c. 1900. Novelty Sign Co., Mansfield, Ohio, 23.5" x 17" x 6". *Courtesy of Dave Monahan.*

Porcelain enamel American Express sign dated May, 1904. Imperial Enamel Co. Ltd., New York (made in England), 13" x 17". *Courtesy of David Justice and Beth Fraser.*

American Express sign dated Oct. 1915. Porcelain enamel, Baltimore Enamel and Novelty Co., Baltimore and 200 5th Ave., New York. 13" x 17". *Courtesy of David Justice and Beth Fraser.*

American Express sign, c. 1920s. Porcelain enamel, Baltimore Enamel and Novelty Company, Baltimore and New York. *Courtesy of David Justice and Beth Fraser.*

Adams Express Company porcelain enamel sign, c. 1880s. 4" x 12". *Courtesy of David Justice and Beth Fraser.*

Wooden two-sided sign for Atlantic and Pacific Telegraph Company, c. 1870-1875. Milk paint finish, 15.5" x 13.5". *Courtesy of Stan Rosenwasser.*

Paper sign for the Howard Dustless Duster, c. 1925. W.F. Powers Co., Lithographer, 27" x 18". *Courtesy of Gary Metz.*

Two-sided exterior sign for American Union Telegraph, c. 1860-1865. Wood with iron hardware, 25.5" x 21". *Courtesy of Stan Rosenwasser.*

One of three known porcelain enamel signs for the Indiana Telephone Co., late 1940s. Two-sided, 18" x 18". *Courtesy of David Justice and Beth Fraser.*

Tin sign for Polly Stamps, trading stamps from the 1950s. Press Sign Co., St. Louis, 18″ x 35″. *Courtesy of Dave Beck.*

Tin sign for Daisy Fly Killer, c. 1880s. Harold Somers, Brooklyn, New York. 13.5″ x 10″. *Courtesy of an anonymous collector.*

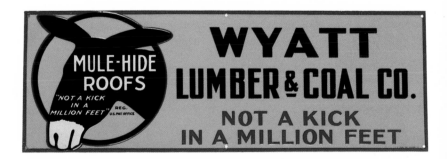

Paper poster for Remington-UMC, c. 1917. 26″ x 18″. *Courtesy of Jay and Joan Millman.*

Wyatt Lumber & Coal tin sign, c. 1940s. R.G. Fishel Inc., Chicago, Illinois, 10″ x 28″. *Courtesy of Dave Beck.*

Porcelain enamel sign for Gold Coin Stoves and Ranges, c. 1895. B.S. Company, Harvey, Illinois, 25.5" x 18.5". *Courtesy of The Olde Mercantile Store.*

Porcelain enamel sign for Greyhound Pickwick Lines, c. 1920s. 29" x 24". *Courtesy of David Justice and Beth Fraser.*

Embossed tin sign for Standard Sewing Machines. 5" x 28". *Courtesy of Joe and Sue Ferriola.*

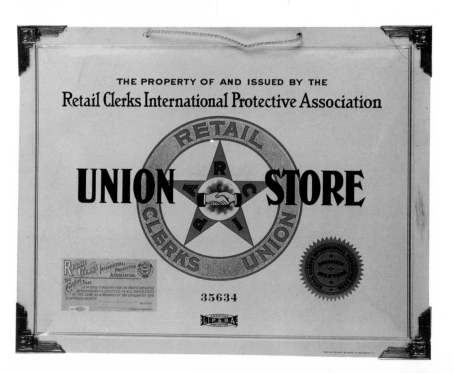

Union sign for a retail store. The Whitehead & Hoag Co., Newark, New Jersey. 8" x 10". *Courtesy of Herb and Elaine Aschendorf.*

An outdoor brass and copper sign for Amdur Leather Co., c. 1920s. 14.5″ x 52″. *Courtesy of Bygones By Blake.*

Painted tin exterior sign for a poultry market, c. 1900. 24″ x 36″. *Courtesy of Stan Rosenwasser.*

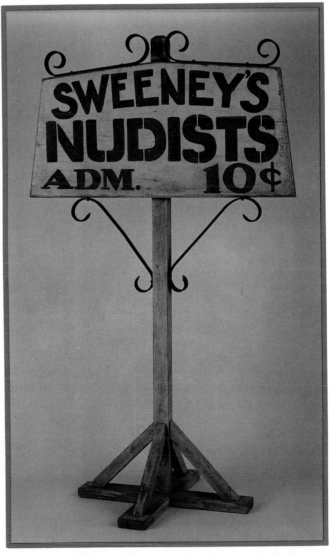

Bush & Lane Piano sign, c. 1910-1919. Wood with transfer letters and image. The Meyercord Co., Chicago, 30.5″ x 25″ with frame. *Courtesy of Bob and Marilou Kay.*

Wood sign with metal brackets for Sweeney's Nudists, c. 1920-1930. 25″ x 43″. *Courtesy of Stan Rosenwasser.*

Cloth poster for RCA tubes, c. 1934. Sweeney Litho Co., Belleville, New Jersey, Rolf Armstrong artist. 39″ x 30.5″. *Courtesy of Jay and Joan Millman.*

Howe Scale paper poster, 31″ x 14.5″ with frame. *Courtesy of Bill Powell, American Arts.*

Two-sided porcelain enamel sign for RCA, cl. 1925-1930. *Courtesy of Gary Metz.*

Paper poster for Winchester Fishing Tackle. 10″ x 20″. *Courtesy of Frank's Antiques.*

Poster for Brown & Bigelow Remembrance Advertising, Saint Paul, Minnesota. Signed Earl Moran. If their purpose was to show the impact of Brown & Bigelow advertising, this poster and the one that follows seem to meet the bill. 30″ x 22″. *Courtesy of Crown Antiques.*

"Life Is Glorious," another paper poster for Brown & Bigelow Remembrance Advertising. 30″ x 22″. *Courtesy of Crown Antiques.*

Rolled tin sign for Amundson Florist, Minneapolis, Minnesota. 14.5″ in diameter. *Courtesy of Hitchner-Morrison.*

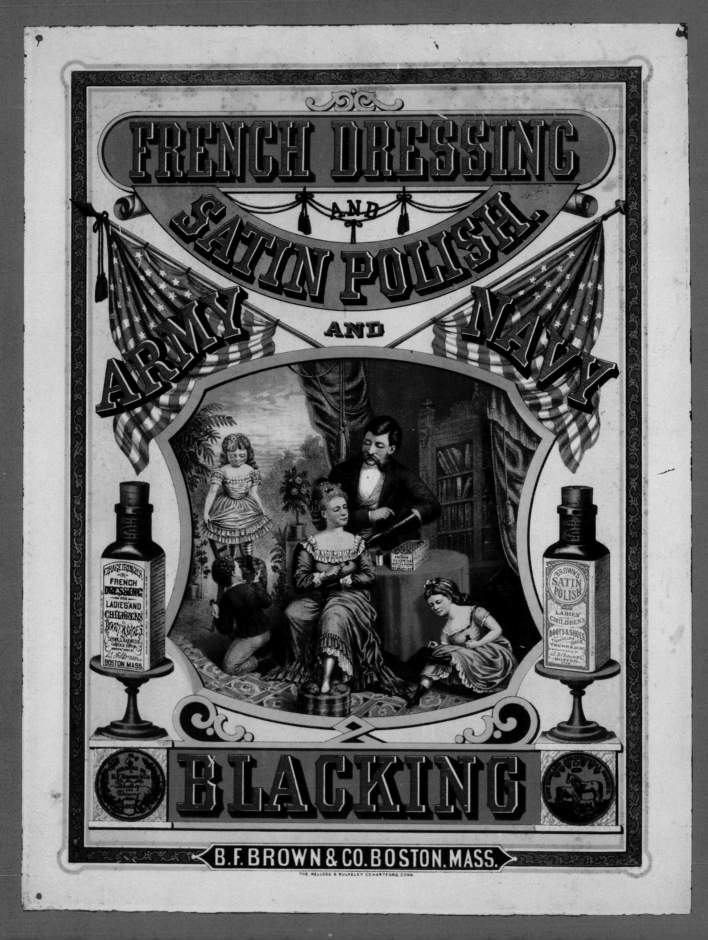

FOOD

Barrel top label for Sleepy Eye Milling Co., c. 1910-1920. Wilmann's Bros. Co., Milwaukee, paper, 16" in diameter. *Courtesy of Phil Perdue.*

Town Crier paper flour box, the Midland Flour Milling Company, Kansas City, c. 1920s. !0" high, 5.5" diameter. *Courtesy of Harold and Elsie Edmondson.*

Barrel top label for Our Pet Flour, Union County Milling Co., Jonesboro, Illinois, c. 1910-1920. Label made by Keller Crescent Co. of paper, 15.5" in diameter. *Courtesy of Phil Perdue.*

Glass front oak display case for Sauer's Best Flavoring and Extracts, c. 1910-1919. 25.5" x 12" x 7". *Courtesy of Joe and Sue Ferriola.*

Tin for Gorton's Cocoanut, by Warner Merritt. The tin was manufactured by Ginna & Co., New York and is 10.75" tall. *Courtesy of Oliver's Auction Gallery.*

Left: W.H. Baker Best Cocoa tin, 3.75" tall. Right: United Happiness Candy Stores one-pound tin, made by Tindeco. Harrison Cady was the artist. *Courtesy of Oliver's Auction Gallery.*

Towles Log Cabin Syrup tin on wheels, c. 1920s. 5" high x 4" wide x 2" deep. *Courtesy of Joe and Sue Ferriola.*

Fairway Oat Flakes box, c. 1910. Twin Cities Wholesale, St. Paul, 10″ x 5.5″. *Courtesy of Harold and Elsie Edmondson.*

Fairway Rolled Oats box from the 1930s. Twin Ports Wholesale, Duluth. 10″ x 5.5″. *Courtesy of Harold and Elsie Edmondson.*

Mama's Choice Rolled Oats box, c. 1910. Samuel Mahon, Ottumwa-Fort Madison, Iowa, 10″ x 5.5″. *Courtesy of Harold and Elsie Edmondson.*

Red Owl Quick Cooking Oats, c. 1940. Red Owl Stores, Minneapolis, 10″ x 5.5″. *Courtesy of Harold and Elsie Edmondson.*

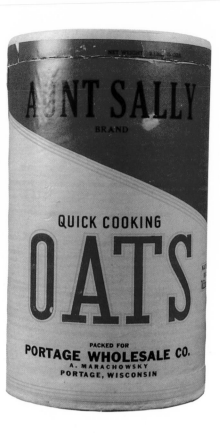

Nice graphics on this Black Bird rolled oats box, c. 1920. 10″ x 5.5″. *Courtesy of Harold and Elsie Edmondson.*

Standby Brownies Rolled Oats, c. 1930s. Fine Foods, Seattle, Washington. 10″ x 5.5″. *Courtesy of Harold and Elsie Edmondson.*

A 1930s Clover Farm rolled oats box. Clover Farm Stores, Cleveland. 10″ x 5.5″. *Courtesy of Harold and Elsie Edmondson.*

Scotch Brand Oats, c. 1930s, by the Quaker Oats Company, Chicago. 10″ x 5.5″. *Courtesy of Harold and Elsie Edmondson.*

Aunt Sally Quick Cooking Oats box, c. 1940s. Portage Wholesale Co., Portage, Wisconsin, 10″ x 5.5″. *Courtesy of Harold and Elsie Edmondson.*

White Villa Rolled Oats, c. 1920s. The Cincinnati Wholesale Groceries, Cincinnati, 10″ x 5.5″. *Courtesy of Harold and Elsie Edmondson.*

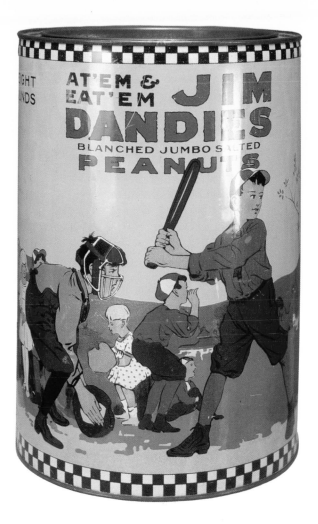

Jim Dandies Peanut tin with a great baseball scene in good strong colors. Bordo Products Co., Chicago, 1916. 11″ tall. *Courtesy of Oliver's Auction Gallery.*

Exton's Oyster and Butter Crackers tin with a lift top and glass front. From Trenton, New Jersey. *Courtesy of Oliver's Auction Gallery.*

Left: Sweet Girl brand peanut butter pail, c. 1920s, 16 ounce size. Geo. Rasmussen Co., Chicago & Minneapolis. The tin was manufactured by American Can Co., 4″ x 3.5″. Only a few of this tin are known to exist. Right: Consumers Best Peanut Butter tin pail, 14 ounce size. Consumer Wholesale Grocers, Chicago. This is the only one known. *Courtesy of Oliver's Auction Gallery.*

Back of a Sweet Girl Peanut Butter pail, showing nice lithography. *Courtesy of Joe and Sue Ferriola.*

Barrel label from F.A. Waidner & Co. sauer kraut. 12″ in diameter. *Courtesy of an anonymous collector.*

White Goose Coffee tin, c. 1920s. The Shuster-Gromly Co., Jeannette, Pennsylvania, 6″ tall. *Courtesy of Joe and Sue Ferriola.*

Lord Calvert Coffee display. Tin, 19″ x 13″ x 6.5″. *Courtesy of Stan Rosenwasser.*

Very early tin from the Great American Tea Company picturing a cockatoo and the factory. 9.75″ tall. *Courtesy of Oliver's Auction Gallery.*

ICE CREAM & CANDY   SOFT DRINKS

Jersey-Creme tin tray, c. 1910. Chas. W. Shonk Co. Litho, Chicago. 12″ in diameter. *Courtesy of Gary Metz.*

Adams Tutti Frutti Gum machine, 32″ tall with an oak case. *Courtesy of Oliver's Auction Gallery.*

Change felt for Luden's Chewing Gum, c. 1905. 11″ x 11.5″. *Courtesy of Jay and Joan Millman.*

NuGrape tin tray, c. 1910. The American Art Works, Inc. Coshocton, Ohio, 13.5″ x 10.5″. *Courtesy of Marcia and Bob Weissman.*

COCA-COLA

Tray for Vernor's Ginger Ale, Detroit, Michigan, c. 1940s. 12″ in diameter. *Courtesy of Gary Metz.*

Early Coca-Cola tray, 1904. Meek Litho, 13″ x 10.5″. Although the tray is faded and scratched, it is still rare and would be considered in fair condition. *Courtesy of Oliver's Auction Gallery.*

Opposite page:

1st Row (l-r): 1914 Coca-Cola tray, Betty oval.; 1909 World's Fair Girl tray, large version; 1909 World's Fair tray, smaller version.

2nd Row (l-r): 1961 Coca-Cola "pansy" tray; 1935 Coca-Cola tray featuring Johnny Weissmuler and Maureen O'sullivan; 1940 Fishing Girl Coca-Cola tray.

3rd Row (l-r): 1930 Telephone Girl Coca-Cola tray; 1929 Coca-Cola tray; 1931 Rockwell Coca-cola tray; 1939 Hayden Coca-Cola tray.

4th Row (l-r): 1926 Golf Coca-Cola tray; 1948 Coca-Cola tray in the rare French version; 1941 Skater Girl Coca-Cola tray; 1933 Francis Dee Coca-Cola tray.

5th Row (l-r): 1927 Coca-Cola tray with bobbed hair girl; 1935 Madge Evans Coca-Cola tray; 1939 Springboard Girl Coke tray in Spanish version; 1942 Girls and Car Coke tray.

Seltzer bottle from Zetz 7-Up Bottling Co., New Orleans. Kaufmann Beverage Co., 12″ x 4″. *Courtesy of Stan Rosenwasser.*

6th Row (l-r): 1937 Coca-Cola tray; 1936 Hostess Girl Coca-Cola tray; 1938 Coca-Cola tray; 1914 Betty rectangular Coca-Cola tray. *Courtesy of Oliver's Auction Gallery.*

Tin tray for American Brewing Company, St. Louis. Chas. W. Shonk Company Litho, Chicago. 12.5″ in diameter. *Courtesy of Hitchner-Morrison.*

Consumer Brewing Company tin tray, c. 1890s. Chas. W. Shonk Litho, Chicago, 12″ in diameter. *Courtesy of Herb and Elaine Aschendorf.*

Oval porcelain tray for Consumer Brewing Company's Thomas Ryan Ales and Lagers. The Baltimore Enamel & Novelty Co., Baltimore, Maryland, 13″ x 16″. *Courtesy of Oliver's Auction Gallery.*

Keeley's Bottled Beer tin tray, 1915. Kaufmann & Strauss, New York, 12″ in diameter. *Courtesy of Gary Metz.*

Oversized Lemp Brewery tin tray, 24″ in diameter. *Courtesy of Oliver's Auction Gallery.*

Tin tray advertising Kaiser Wilhelm Bitters, c. 1910. H.D. Beach Co., Coshocton, Ohio, 14″ x 10″. *Courtesy of Harold and Elsie Edmondson.*

Oversized Lemp Brewery tin tray manufactured by the Haeusermann Metal Mfg. Co., 24″ in diameter. *Courtesy of Oliver's Auction Gallery.*

Papier mâche lion for Löwenbräu Beer, 34″ tall. *Courtesy of Oliver's Auction Gallery.*

Moerlein Old Jug Lager King Bier pint bottle, c. 1900-1905. Christian and Moerlein, Cincinnati, Ohio. In the hands of the cherubs in this version are nursing bottles. In the original bottles the babies had beer bottles. 5.75″ tall. *Courtesy of Fil and Robbie Graf.*

National Bohemian display (red), Nation Brewing Co., Baltimore & Detroit, 1960. Plastic, 8.25″. *Courtesy of Fil and Robbie Graf.*

National Bohemian display (white), National Brewing Co., Baltimore, Maryland, Orlando, Florida, Detroit, Michigan. Chalkware, 6.75″, 1956-61. *Courtesy of Fil and Robbie Graf.*

Plaster Oertel's counter display, c. 1950s. 16.5″ x 11″. *Courtesy of Mike and Doris Brown.*

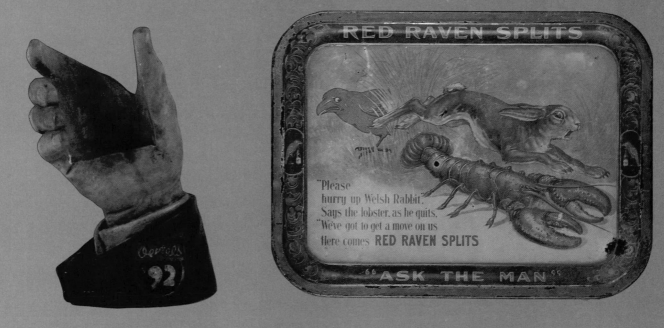

Plaster Oertel's counter display, 1940s. 11″ x 5″. *Courtesy of Mike and Doris Brown.*

Red Raven Splits tin tray, c. 1900. Chas. W. Shonk, Chicago, 10.5″ x 14″. *Courtesy of Herb and Elaine Aschendorf.*

E. Robinson's Sons Pilsener Beer tin tray, 1910-1919. A common tray, it was produced with different rims. 12" diameter. *Courtesy of Herb and Elaine Aschendorf.*

Left: Welz and Zerweck, 16.5" oval beer tray, featuring a great polo scene in the background. Litho by Haeusermann M.M. Co., New York, Chicago. Right: Peter Doelger oval beer tray, 16.5". Litho by Haeusermann. *Courtesy of Oliver's Auction Gallery.*

1st Row (l-r): Heim Beer tray, 16.5" x 13.5". Bairisch Factory scene; Peter Hand Brewery Co., Chicago, Illinois. Chas. W. Shonk litho, Chicago.

2nd Row (l-r): Tin Baker's Chocolate tray, 16.5" x 14"; super oval tray for Narragansett Brewing Co., 22.5" x 16.5"; Welz and Zerweck Brewery tray, Brooklyn, New York, 13.5" x 16.5".

3rd Row (l-r): Liberty Beer, Rochester, New York, tin tray, 12" in diameter. Charles Shonk Litho; Rolled tin White Rock sign, Charles Shonk, litho; Champagne Velvet beer tray, Terre Haute Brewing Co., Chas. Shonk Litho; Zipp's Cherri-O tray in near mint condition. 12" diameter, H.D. Beach, Coshocton, Ohio.

"The City Cousin" tin tray for the Ruff Brewing Co., Quincy, Illinois, c. 1908. Signed by the artist, Carl Hirschberg. 13" x 13". *Courtesy of Marcia and Bob Weissman.*

WHISKEY AND OTHER SPIRITS

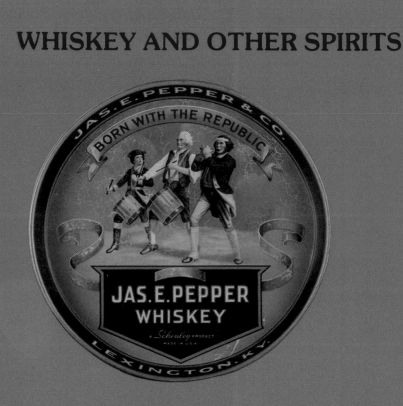

Jas. E. Pepper Whiskey tray, c. 1920s. Electro Chemical Engraving Co., Inc., New York, New York. 12″ in diameter. *Courtesy of Mike and Doris Brown.*

Oversized Biscuit Cognac bottle, glass 20 inches tall. *Courtesy of Oliver's Auction Gallery.*

Mumm's Extra Rye Whiskey tray, c. 1920s. Kaufmann & Strauss Co., New York. Tin, 12″ in diameter. *Courtesy of Mike and Doris Brown.*

A group of etched advertising beer and shot glasses. The shortest is 2.5″ tall x 2″ in diameter. The largest is 4″ tall x 2.5″ in diameter. *Courtesy of Oliver's Auction Gallery.*

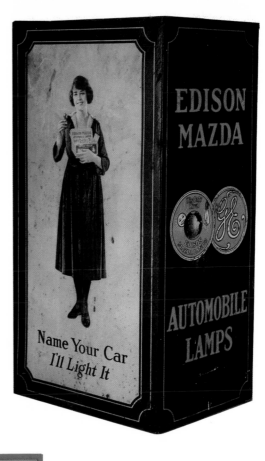

Display shelf for Bonney and Champion Vises. Cast iron and wood, 15" x 18" x 9.5". *Courtesy of Stan Rosenwasser*.

Metal storage case for Mazda Automobile Lamps. 23.25" x 12" x 12". *Courtesy of Oliver's Auction Gallery*.

Sweetheart Soap baby in a bassinet. 22" x 16.5" x 33". *Courtesy of Road Runner Antiques*.

TIP TRAYS

Tin tip tray for Page's Ice Cream, 6" x 4.5". *Courtesy of Joe and Sue Ferriola.*

"Have some Junket" tip tray, Chr. Hansen's Laboratory, Little Falls, New York. 4" in diameter. *Courtesy of Joe and Sue Ferriola.*

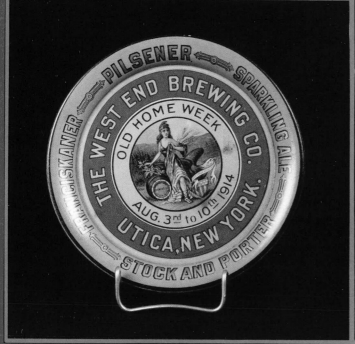

West End Brewing Co., Utica, New York tip tray. Tin, 4.25" in diameter. The Hausermann's Litho, New York & Chicago. *Courtesy of Joe and Sue Ferriola.*

Wrigley's Soap tip tray, Wrigley Manufacturing, Philadelphia. Made by the American Can Company. 3.5" in diameter. *Courtesy of Joe and Sue Ferriola.*

IV.
Advertising in Miniature: Smalls

Tip tray for the Leisy Brewing Company, Peoria, Illinois. Kaufmann & Strauss, New York. 5.25″ in diameter. *Courtesy of Joe and Sue Ferriola.*

Moxie tip tray featuring a pretty lady. H.D. Beach Co., Coshocton, Ohio. 6″ in diameter. *Courtesy of Joe and Sue Ferriola.*

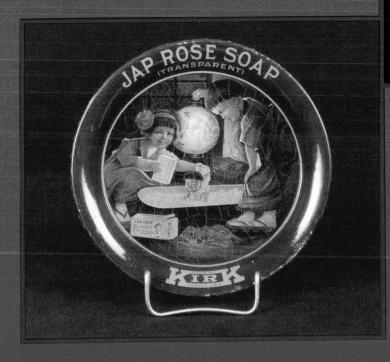

Kirk Company's Jap Rose Soap tip tray. Hausermann's Litho, New York, 4.25″ in diameter. *Courtesy of Joe and Sue Ferriola.*

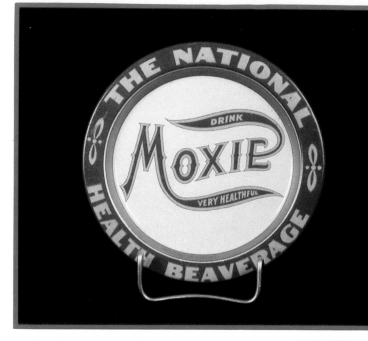

Tin Moxie tip tray with the foxtail tip to the logo. Chas. Shonk, Chicago, 3.5". *Courtesy of Joe and Sue Ferriola.*

Doelger Beer tip tray, 5.5" in diameter. *Courtesy of Joe and Sue Ferriola.*

MIRRORS

Tip tray advertising Ruhstaller's Gilt Edge Lager, Sacramento, California. Kaufmann & Strauss, New York, 4.25" in diameter. *Courtesy of Joe and Sue Ferriola.*

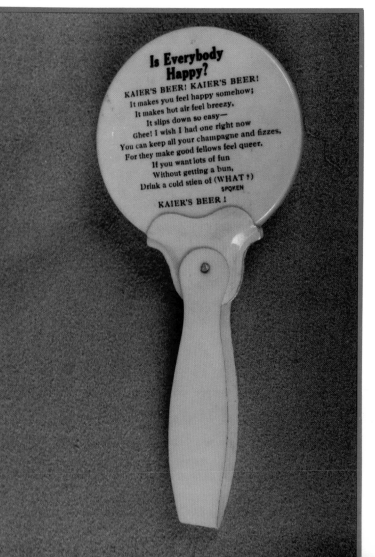

Folding mirror of celluloid and glass for Kaier's Beer. 4.75" x 2". *Courtesy of Jay and Joan Millman.*

This beautiful lady is advertising "Oh My" The Souvenir Pop Corn on the back of this pocket mirror. "Oh My" was made by the National Candy Company. The mirror was made Whitehead & Hoag, c. 1904. 1.75" in diameter. *Courtesy of Jay and Joan Millman.*

The Hazelton Hotel in Taunton, Massachusetts is advertised on this mirror with the beautiful lady. 2" in diameter. *Courtesy of Jay and Joan Millman.*

A rather plain pocket mirror for the Fried and Reineman Packing Company. The mirror was made by Whitehead & Hoag. 1.75" x 2.75". *Courtesy of Jay and Joan Millman.*

Another simple mirror for the Arnholt & Schaefer Brewing Company, Philadelphia. Whitehead and Hoag, Newark, New Jersey, 1.75" in diameter. *Courtesy of Jay and Joan Millman.*

This mirror is showing its age somewhat, but it is still beautiful. For "The Juliette," a feminine version of the "Romeo" slipper. Boston, 2.75″ x 1.75″. *Courtesy of Jay and Joan Millman.*

A nicely done mirror for the Sharpless Separator Company, West Chester, Pennsylvania. 2.75″ x 1.75″. *Courtesy of Jay and Joan Millman.*

The tradition of dancing on a boat in Boston Harbor continues to this day. This mirror advertises the S.S. Jack O'Lantern with "Dancing Every Evening on Board." 2.75″ x 1.75″. *Courtesy of Jay and Joan Millman.*

This beautiful lady is advertising Seely's Celeste, The New Perfume." 1.75″. *Courtesy of Jay and Joan Millman.*

Mirror advertising Mascot Crushed Cut Tobacco. Whitehead & Hoag, 2.25". *Courtesy of Jay and Joan Millman.*

Art Stove Company of Detroit used this mirror to promote its Laurel Stoves. Presumably the woman is Laurel. 2.75" x 1.75". *Courtesy of Jay and Joan Millman.*

BLOTTERS

A 1912 blotter for the Eckerson Company, Jersey City, New Jersey. Whitehead & Hoag Company, Newark. Celluloid and paper, 8" x 3". *Courtesy of Jay and Joan Millman.*

The woman on this blotter may look familiar. She appeared without the flowers on the mirror for Seely's Celeste. This piece advertises Mould's Women's wear, Reading, Pennsylvania. Bastian Brothers, Rochester, New York. 3" x 6". *Courtesy of Jay and Joan Millman.*

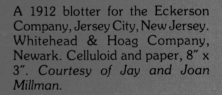

Blotter advertising Kingan's Reliable brand meats, Indianapolis. Whitehead & Hoag Co., Newark. 3" x 7.5". *Courtesy of Jay and Joan Millman.*

Another blotter for Kingan's meats. Whitehead & Hoag, 8" x 3.25". *Courtesy of Jay and Joan Millman.*

Blotter and 1922 calendar advertising the Southern Steamship Company. Manufactured by Pilgrim Specialty Co., Malden, Massachusetts. 3" x 7.75". *Courtesy of Jay and Joan Millman.*

Parisian Novelty Company, Chicago made this geometric design blotter for the Portland Trust Co., Portland, Connecticut. 2.75" x 7". *Courtesy of Jay and Joan Millman.*

Celluloid on tin blotter for the High Point Oil Company, Indiana. 7.5" x 3.5". *Courtesy of Jay and Joan Millman.*

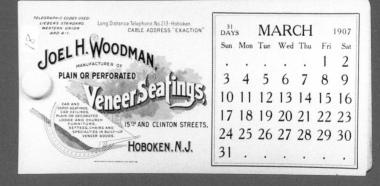

Calendar and blotter for the Joel H. Woodman Seating Company, Hoboken, New Jersey. Whitehead & Hoag, 6.75" 3.25". *Courtesy of Jay and Joan Millman.*

MEMOS AND CALENDARS

Here she is again, this time adorning a calendar and memorandum book for 1925. Celluloid and paper, 3" x 2". *Courtesy of Jay and Joan Millman.*

A blotter advertising the advertiser, c. 1903. "The Whitehead & Hoag Co., makers of advertising novelties, badges, celluloid buttons, signs, metal specialties, gold and enamel emblems, leather goods, art calendars, &c." *Courtesy of Jay and Joan Millman.*

Memo book by Whitehead and Hoag, 1905. Celluloid and paper, 5" x 2.5". *Courtesy of Jay and Joan Millman.*

Memo and Calendar for Fleischman's Yeast, 1911. Made by Bastian Brothers, Rochester, New York. Celluloid and paper, 3" x 2". *Courtesy of Jay and Joan Millman.*

151

Memo book for Mlle. Claff's La Parisienne Corsets, Boston. Bastian Brothers, Rochester, New York, 3.75″ x 2.25″. *Courtesy of Jay and Joan Millman.*

Memo pad for the Schissler College of Business, Norristown, Pennsylvania, 1902. Whitehead and Hoag, 4.75″ x 2″. *Courtesy of Jay and Joan Millman.*

Celluloid notebook with nice graphics for Hoffman House Pure Rye, The Hamburger Co., Chicago. 5″ x 3″. *Courtesy of Oliver's Auction Gallery.*

MATCHSAFES

Brass and paper matchsafe advertising the M. Stachelberg & Co., Havana Cigar Makers. 1.5″ x 1.75″. *Courtesy of Jay and Joan Millman.*

Plated brass matchsafe with heavily embossed decoration advertising the John Hauck Brewing Company, Cincinnati. 3″ x 1.5″. *Courtesy of Jay and Joan Millman.*

...nd celluloid matchsafe for the John Hohenadel
..., Philadelphia. 3" x 1.5". *Courtesy of Jay and Joan*

Brass matchsafe for Banquet Hall and Bouq...
manufactured by M. Foster & Co., New York.
Courtesy of Jay and Joan Millman.

...matchsafe for Pierce's Nine Cigars, Boston. 2.5" x
...rtesy of Jay and Joan Millman.

Embossed matchsafe for the Indianapolis Brewing Company. 3" x 1.5". *Courtesy of Jay and Joan Millman.*

Heavily decorated match-safe for the Pan American Exposition, 1901. 3" x 1.75". *Courtesy of Jay and Joan Millman.*

Heavily embossed 1904 matchsafe advertising the International Tailoring Co. 1.75″ x 2.5″. *Courtesy of Jay and Joan Millman.*

MATCH HOLDERS AND STRIKERS

A match holder advertising J. C. Stevens' Old Judson drink. Tin, manufactured by Foster M. Rieder, Kansas City, Missouri, and Savage Manufacturing Co., New York. 5″ x 3.5″. *Courtesy of Joe and Sue Ferriola.*

Cribben & Sexton's Universal Stoves and Ranges is advertised on this tin match holder. 5″ x 3.5″. *Courtesy of Joe and Sue Ferriola.*

Match holder for Green's August Flower and Boschee's German Syrup, both made in Woodbury, New Jersey. August Flower was a remedy for dyspepia, indigestion, and liver complaint, while German Syrup "cured" coughs, colds and consumption. Cardboard, 8″ x 4.5″. *Courtesy of Joe and Sue Ferriola.*

Tin Moxie match holder. 7" x 2.5". *Courtesy of Joe and Sue Ferriola.*

Tin match holder advertising the Keely Stove Company, Philadelphia and Columbia. Ginna & Co., New York, 7.5" x 5". *Courtesy of Joe and Sue Ferriola.*

Milwaukee Harvesting Machines match holder. Tin, manufactured by Chas. W. Shonk, Chicago. 5.5" x 4". *Courtesy of Joe and Sue Ferriola.*

Solarine Metal Polish match holder. Tin, 5" x 3.5". *Courtesy of Joe and Sue Ferriola.*

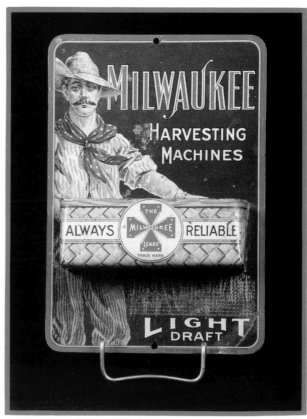

Die-cut and embossed match holder for De Laval milk separator. Manufactured by the L.T. Savage Co., New York. 6.5" x 7.5". *Courtesy of Joe and Sue Ferriola.*

Embossed tin match holder for the Columbia Mill Co., Minneapolis. 5.5" x 2.25". *Courtesy of Joe and Sue Ferriola.*

PEN KNIVES

Pocket knife by J.H. Henckel, Germany, for the English China Clays Sales Corporation. 3.25". *Courtesy of Jay and Joan Millman.*

Pen knife advertising the Home Insurance Co., New York, Chester M. Cloud, agent. The W. & H. Co., Newark(?). 2.25". *Courtesy of Jay and Joan Millman.*

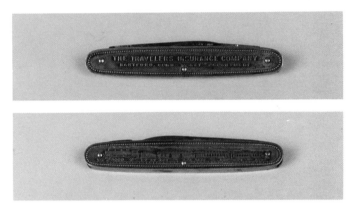

Another W. & H. Company knife, this time for the Traveler Insurance Company, Hartford, Connecticut. The name is on one side and a nicely embossed train on the other. 3.25". *Courtesy of Jay and Joan Millman.*

MISCELLANEOUS

Cigar cutter advertising Que Placer High Grade Mild Cigars. J. Hastruck, New York. 1.75" x 1". *Courtesy of Jay and Joan Millman.*

Pencil clips advertising Star Brand Shoes and the Association of Machinists and Aerospace Workers. *Courtesy of Jay and Joan Millman.*

Celluloid luggage tag advertising the Hotel Chamberlain, Fort Monroe, Virginia. 1.5″ x 2.5″. *Courtesy of Jay and Joan Millman.*

Celluloid pinochle score keeper advertising the International Tailoring Co., New York and Chicago. Whitehead and Hoag, Newark, 1.5″ x 3″. *Courtesy of Jay and Joan Millman.*

Cast iron pot scraper advertising the Tens Cokenny (?) Co., coffees and sugar. 1″ x 4″ x 2″. *Courtesy of Joe and Sue Ferriola.*

V.
Calendars, Thermometers, and Other Advertising Novelties

CALENDARS

Beautiful calendar for Cape Brewing & Ice Company, Cape Girardeau, Missouri, 1908. Die-cut cardboard, 21.5" x 14.5". *Courtesy of The Hug Collection.*

1929 Coca-Cola calendar. *Courtesy of Oliver's Auction Gallery.*

Humorous calendar for Grace Mills, Warsaw Milling Company, Warsaw, Illinois. The weather forecast on the wall is prophetic to the situation: "Violent local disturbances, cyclonic storm centre rapidly approaching. Thunder and lightning. Terrific gusts. Torrents of scalding water. Unparalleled meteorological phenomenon. Rainy Blanket." *Courtesy of Dennis and Gloria Healzer.*

Paper calendar for the Hamm's Brewery, St. Paul, Minnesota, 1903. 30" x 22". *Courtesy of Dave Beck.*

The original art work for a De Laval Separator calendar, 1917. Forbes Litho, Boston, 40.5" x 22". *Courtesy of The Hug Collection.*

Detmer Woolens calendar, 1919. Paper, 32.5" x 20.5", and printed with the retailers name, Andrew Wils, Rapid River, Michigan. *Courtesy of Dick and Katie Bucht.*

Dutch Boy calendar, paper, 35.5″ x 14.5″. *Courtesy of Herb and Elaine Aschendorf.*

William A. Jones Calendar, 1910. Kemper-Thomas Co., Cincinnati, Ohio, 21.5″ x 13.5″. *Courtesy of Joe and Sue Ferriola.*

Paper Lowell Fertilizer Calendar, 1913. 25″ x 12″. *Courtesy of Sue and Ted Allen.*

Lambertville Rubber Footwear calendar, 1914. Ketterlinus, Philadelphia, 36″ x 23″. *Courtesy of Gary Metz.*

Lambertville Rubber Footwear Calendar, 1920. Ketterlinus, Philadelphia, copyright 1916, 36″ x 23″. *Courtesy of Gary Metz.*

Pepsi calendar featuring a beautiful woman, 1941. Paper, 22.5" x 14.5". *Courtesy of Gary Metz.*

1919 Winchester Calendar with art work by Richard Amick. F.A. Berger Company, 38.5" x 20". *Courtesy of John Kemler with Craig Grotzmaker and Dave Delongchamp.*

THERMOMETERS

Souvenir from the National Canner's Association meeting in Buffalo, New York, 1907. Graphics on both sides and a thermometer on one edge. It is filled with sand and was probably given out as a paper weight. *Courtesy of Oliver's Auction Gallery.*

Thermometer for The Courier-Journal/The Louisville Times, late 1920s. Used at A.T. Schreiber Drugstore. 18" in diameter. *Courtesy of Mike and Doris Brown.*

Burke's Superior Ale thermometer, 1938-1940. Burke's was brewed by Arthur Guinness & Sons. The thermometer was manufactured by Place & Place, New York, 8.5" x 8.5". *Courtesy of Jay and Joan Millman.*

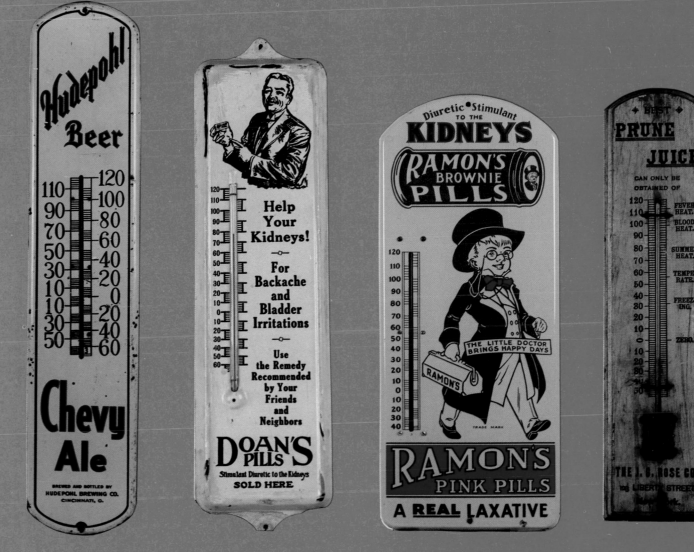

Hudepohl Beer thermometer, c. 1945. Porcelain enamel, 37" x 8". *Courtesy of Fil and Robbie Graf.*

Doan's Pills thermometer, c. 1910. Porcelain enamel, 24" x 6.5" *Courtesy of Herb and Elaine Aschendorf.*

Ramon's Brownie Pills thermometer, late 1930s. Tin, 21" x 9". *Courtesy of Gary Metz.*

Thermometer advertising J.G. Rose's "Best" Prune Juice, c. 1915. Manufactured by R. Hoehn Co., New York, 21" x 5.5". *Courtesy of Herb and Elaine Aschendorf.*

Pie-shaped None Such thermometer from the early 1920s. 9.5 inches in diameter, it is marked Merrell-Soule Co., Syracuse and Standard Thermometer, Peabody, Massachusetts. The back is shaped as a pie tin. *Courtesy of Dennis and Gloria Healzer.*

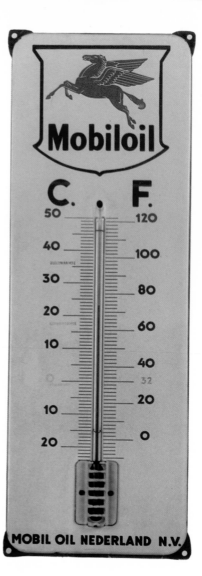

Mobiloil Thermometer, c. 1930s. Porcelain enamel, 23" x 8". *Courtesy of Kim and Mary Kokles.*

Hire's Root Beer thermometer. Tin, 28" x 8". *Courtesy of Bob Thomas.*

CLOCKS

Tin Coca-Cola clock with an electric movement by General Electric. 18" in diameter. *Courtesy of Al Wilson.*

L: Advertising clock for Kleenatub and Wrigley's Scouring Soap. It has a pendulum and key, and a 34″ tall oak case. R: A Baird advertising clock for Jolly Tar, Old Honesty, Plank Road, Pastime, Five Bros., and Boot Jack Tobacco, products of the John Finzer Tobacco Manufacturers, Louisville, Kentucky. It has a key and pendulum. *Courtesy of Oliver's Auction Gallery.*

Very rare U.S. Tire Co. wall clock, c. 1910-1920. Litho on wood, 18″ in diameter. *Courtesy of Kim and Mary Kokles.*

MISCELLANEOUS

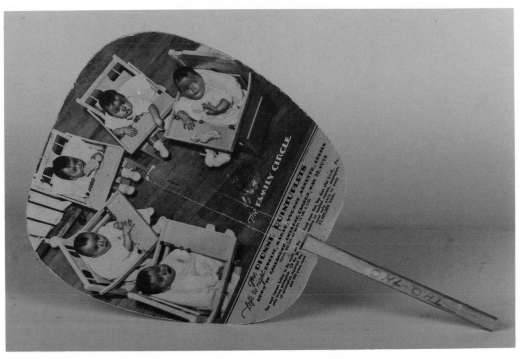

Dionne Quintuplets advertising fan, advertising the Chatfield Equity Exchange Company, Chatfield, Ohio. Manufactured circa 1935 by the Brown & Bigelow Company. 14″ x 8.5″.

Phillips 66 fan advertising Van's Service Station, Downtown Fairbury, Illinois. Wood and cardboard, 14″ x 8.5″. *Courtesy of Koehler Bros., Inc.—The General Store, Lafayette, Indiana.*

A.S. Valentine & Son, Betsy Ross cigar cutter, patented 1902. Cast iron and glass, 8.5″ x 8″. *Courtesy of Gary Metz.*

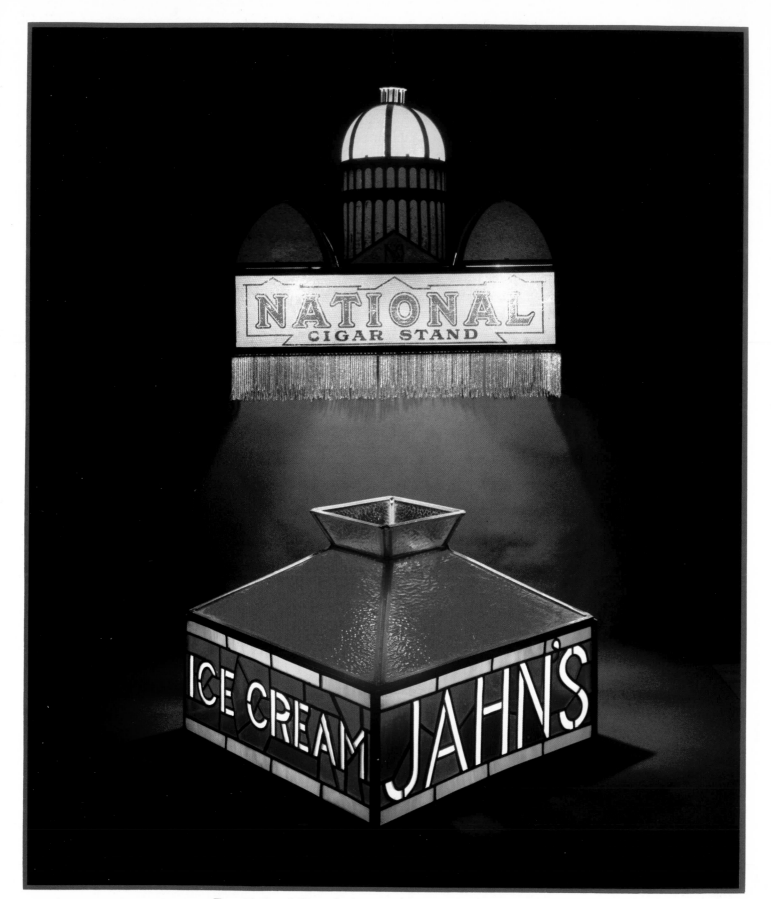

Top: National Cigar lantern in the rare mica version, not glass. Very nice. Bottom: Nice leaded glass shade for Jahn's Ice Cream. *Courtesy of Oliver's Auction Gallery.*

Chevrolet puzzle, c. 1932. Cardboard, 9.5" x 16.5".
Courtesy of Herbert Ramsey.

Crystal Spring Brewing Co., stoneware
match holder, well-marked. 6.5" in diameter.
Courtesy of Oliver's Auction Gallery.

Ceramic mug advertising Bowman's
Department Store, Harrisburg,
Pennsylvania. Marked Haynes, Baltimore,
5" x 3.5". *Courtesy of Gary Metz.*

Self-framing porcelain portrait of Mrs. [Grover?] Cleveland advertising Spark's Perfect Health, c. 1890s. Given by the Spark's Medicine Co., Camden, New Jersey. Manufactured by Robert H. Payne, Porceline Show Cards, Camden, New Jersey. 16.5″ x 11″. *Courtesy of Kim and Mary Kokles.*

Sample bridge table from Samson, c. 1930s. 30″ x 30″. *Courtesy of Stan Rosenwasser.*

174

Full color Coca-Cola advertisement which ran in the Sunday Magazine of the Sunday Record Herald, May 19, 1907. *Courtesy of an anonymous collector.*

Bibliography

Burns, R.M., and Bradley, W.W. *Protective Coatings for Metals*. New York: Reinhold Publishing Corporation, 1967.

Congdon-Martin, Douglas. *Country Store Collectibles*. West Chester: Schiffer Publishing Ltd., 1990.

Duling, Ed. "Coshocton Famous for its Advertising Trays," *Antique Week*, Vol. 24, No. 8. Knightstown, Indiana: Mayhill Publications, May 20, 1991.

Gallo, Max. *The Poster in History*. New York: American Heritage Publishing Co., Inc., 1974.

Holme, Bryan. *Advertising: Reflections of a Century*. New York: Viking Press, 1982.

Hornsby, Peter R.G. *Decorated Biscuit Tins*. West Chester: Schiffer Publishing Ltd., 1984.

Hornung, Clarence P., and Johnson, Fridolf. *200 Years of American Graphic Art*. New York: George Braziller, 1976.

Klug, Ray. *Antique Advertising Encyclopedia*. Gas City, Indiana: L-W Promotions, 1978.

Antique Advertising Encyclopedia. West Chester: Schiffer Publishing Ltd., 1985.

Margolin, Victor, Brichta, Ira, and Brichta, Vivian. *The Promise and the Product: 200 Years of American Advertising Posters*. New York: Macmillan Publishing Co., Inc., 1979.

Porzio, Domenico, Editor. *Lithography: 200 Years of Art, History, and Technique*. New York: Harry N. Abrams, Inc., Publishers, 1983.

Richter, Joachim F. *Antique Enamels for Collectors*. West Chester: Schiffer Publishing, Ltd., 1990.

Senefelder, Alois. *A Complete Course of Lithography*. New York: Da Capo Press, 1968.

"Shaw-Barton: The Story of a Business...and an Industry." Circa 1980.

Wood, James Playsted. *The Story of Advertising*. New York: The Ronald Press Company, 1958.